CW01641962

THIRD EDI

ASHTAVAKRA GITA

The Ultimate Solace

Verses of Self-Realization with an Enlightening Commentary by

Harsha

Ashtavakra Gita: The Ultimate Solace - Third Edition by Harsha (Harshvardhan Yardi)

Published by Harsha (Harshvardhan Yardi)

First Edition 2017
Second Edition 2020
Third Edition 2022

For Third Edition:
ISBN 978-93-5659-823-2 (eBook)
ISBN 978-93-5679-965-3 (trade paperback)
ISBN 978-93-5680-228-5 (hard cover)

Cover & Interior Design: Harsha
Set in Bodoni Bk Bt.

Trade Paperback and Hard Cover:
Printed and bound outside India by Amazon KDP Print
Printed and bound in India by Pothi

Contents

Praise For The Book

"As humanity searches for a more authentic narrative, we only need to look at the wisdom of our past. Harsha has done just that. By mindfully translating the wisdom of the *Vedas*, he has brought a gift from our past, into the present ... which is that humanity can more fully embody its spiritual truth.
Well done, Harsha!
Thank you for this wonderful gift."

– Les Jensen, Author, spiritual podcast host, speaker, coach and founder of new human living. Newhumanliving.com

Acknowledgements

I express my sincere gratitude to Bhagyashree Joshi, Pune, for the line editing work she has done on this edition.

I remain deeply appreciative of my following students for the love and readiness they showed in suggesting small edits; and, for becoming the beta readers of this book:

1. Mike Broadbent, Pennsylvania, United States.
2. Dr. Alka Tyagi, Associate Professor, Delhi University.
3. Akshai Narain, Cotswolds, United Kingdom.

To Begin With

Free of Three, Yet, Fills the Three,
To That Sentient Being,
I Surrender.

About The Author

Harsha left behind his flourishing career as a software engineer in his mid-twenties, and became a dedicated spiritual seeker.

He spent a decade of intense struggle doing spiritual practices and austerities in the raw conditions of Himalayas.

During this period, he also learned the original Sanskrit scriptures of Indian Philosophy in a traditional monastery.

Currently, he teaches various systems of Indian philosophy, and guides spiritual seekers.

His interactive lectures on spirituality and self-realization are well received among his students across various countries.

He has traveled to countries like Russia, Nepal and India to deliver interactive discourses on spirituality and self-realization.

To discover his other works, please visit: www.ajatsrishti.com

Story Of Ashtavakra

There was a sage in ancient India, named Kahola.

He used to recite holy *Vedic* hymns every morning; but he used to make mistakes in his recitation.

One morning, while he was reciting the hymns, his *yet to be born son* pointed out the mistakes from the womb of his wife.

Kahola became angry and cursed the son that the son shall be born with a deformed body.

The son was born a few months later. As per the curse, he had eight deformities in the body. Therefore, he was named *Ashtavakra: A person with eight bents.*

Later on in his life, *Ashtavakra* went on to become a great spiritual master.

During that period, the country was ruled by a king named Janaka.

Janaka was a good ruler and a pious person.

One night, while he was asleep on his royal bed, he had a dream in which he saw himself as a beggar who was hungry for three days, and who was getting humiliated by the passers-by; and when he managed to get a little food in his bowl, a pair of bulls came fighting near him and stubbed the bowl.

Terrified by this nightmare, Janaka woke up.

As he opened his eyes, he found himself sleeping on the royal bed that was surrounded by royal amenities and servants.

He became perplexed, and thought: '*Which one is the real phenomenon: this waking state world or that dream world? Which one is the real me: this king or that beggar?*'

The very next morning, he called a meeting of scholars in his courtroom. The scholars gathered in the courtroom.

Janaka narrated the dream to them, and asked them certain questions about the reality of the phenomenal world, and that of the *real self*.

The scholars debated among themselves for hours, and tried to answer Janaka's questions, but none of them were able to give a convincing answer to him.

Just then, Janaka noticed the arrival of an unusual looking person in the courtroom.

He was the great sage – *Ashtavakra*.

Janaka told him the dream, and asked him the same questions.

Ashtavakra smiled and replied, "O Janaka, neither this waking state world is a reality nor is this king your *real self*.

Neither that dream world was a reality nor was that beggar your *real self*.

The waking state, the dream state and the deep sleep replace each other, therefore, none of these states can be the real phenomenon.

In the same way, the form of the waking state subject, the form of the dream state subject and the form of the deep sleep subject replace each other, therefore, none of them can be the *real self*.

The reality can only be that existence which can never get replaced, either by another state or by another form.

There is indeed one such *existence* that does not get replaced; and which remains ever present as the foundation of the transitory phenomena of the waking, dreaming and deep sleep states.

That same existence remains ever present as the existential foundation of the transitory forms of the subjects of these three states.

That existence is a formless and un-qualitative *being*, called *Brahman.* It is one without any second, and it is the only reality. That *Brahman* is your real self. You are that."

About The Book

Ashtavakra Gita, also known as the *Song of Ashtavakra*, is a Sanskrit scripture which has two hundred and ninety-eight verses spread across twenty chapters.

These verses present a dialogue that took place between Sage Ashtavakra and King Janaka in ancient times.

A story of how this dialogue took place goes as follows:

King Janaka was ruling over a part of ancient India. His kingdom was bountiful and his subjects were happy.

Once he went to the hermitage of sage Ashtavakra to seek blessings from him.

After their brief meeting, Janaka got up from his seat, bowed in reverence to the sage and turned around to start on his return journey.

Ashtavakra followed him to the doorstep.

Janaka went near his royal horse, grabbed the horse leash in his hand, and placed his left foot in the left side stirrup attached to the horse saddle.

He was about to climb the horse when, suddenly, a thought gripped his mind.

He turned his face around, and asked Ashtavakra, "Do you have a means that can liberate me before I place my other foot in the other stirrup?"

Ashtavakra, who did have such a means, narrated the spiritual wisdom to Janaka through the couplets known as *Ashtavakra Gita - the Song of Ashtavakra.*

These couplets present the dialogue that took place between the two.

This dialogue provides a great solace to spiritual seekers and to other ordinary mortals who often try to find the means of happiness outside of themselves ignoring the ever-blissful nature of their *real self*.

In this dialogue, Ashtavakra repeatedly narrates the fact that an un-qualitative formless existence is the ultimate reality; and that is our *real self*.

In this book, the author has translated the original Sanskrit verses of the Ashtavakra Gita into English language. In doing so, he has tried to preserve the poetic form of the verses. He has also written an enlightening commentary on each of these verses to explain the perspective and the logic of the philosophy of non-dualism.

This book enlightens the readers about their *real self*, paving the way for their *self-realization*.

Just as the commentary, the verses in themselves also provide a great solace to the reader's mind.

The commentary contains a *Doubt-Answer model* that helps the reader clear his doubts vis-ā-vis the logic of non-dualism.

It takes the readers into a deep ocean of spiritual wisdom by unfolding the concepts and the logic of non-dualism.

Author's Note

The fundamental objective that drives our activity is: *more happiness.*

We may articulate this objective differently, but the basic motivation stays the same: *to have more happiness, and preferably, to have eternal happiness.*

During our lifetime, we remain occupied with our dealings on the material plane in pursuit of that *more happiness,* but we realize that those dealings cannot give us eternal happiness.

Therefore, we start looking for a spiritual solution.

There is a spiritual solution that can help us attain eternal happiness, and that solution is called *self-realization.*

The term *self-realization* implies *doubtless understanding of our real self,* who happens to be the formless, un-qualitative, omnipresent and non-dual existence.

Ashtavakra Gita imparts an ultimate and uncompromising wisdom that facilitates us to have *self-realization* in a direct and daring manner.

In this book, I have made a sincere effort to convey this highest form of spiritual wisdom in the English language, by translating the original Sanskrit verses of *Ashtavakra Gita* into English; and by writing a commentary on each of the verses.

I have neither included the Sanskrit text of the verses nor its transliterated script; so that we can maintain our focus on the message of sage Ashtavakra; instead of having distractions caused by the script.

In this book, the word *mind* refers to *the mental functions which reinforce ignorance*; and it does not necessarily refer to the material fabric of the mind, unless specified so in the context.

Certain words such as *subjective intervention*, *personal intervention* and *psychological intervention* refer to *the interaction of an ignorant subject with the world, done with an intention of extracting pleasure out of that interaction.*

Certain terms such as *wise one*, *enlightened one*, *self-realized person* or *enlightened person* refer to *a person who has realized the formless non-dual existence as his real self.*

Some of the verses may sound repetitive, but they are not cliches; on the contrary, they reveal the beauty of *Ashtavakra Gita*, because each and every verse of it can be a scripture in itself.

I would advise the readers to keep their *takeaway* of this book confined to the *plane of understanding*; instead of trying to implement it on the *activity plane* by means of practice.

This wisdom serves its purpose best when it is allowed to remain at the *plane of understanding* alone; and not when it is dragged to the activity plane; and there is a reason for that:

The purpose of this wisdom is to bring a *realization* to us that our *real self* is the *formless existence* which is an *omnipresent being*.

This *realization* is not supposed to be manufactured by us by means of activity-based practice because that would amount to the subjective intervention from our side, and the moment we try to make subjective intervention, we already lose the plot by means of our assumption that *our self is an individual subject.*

Therefore, we should let the wisdom remove our doubts, and then the *realization* dawns on its own, because this *realization* is *not* a metaphysical transformation, but it is merely an understanding that brings clarity to us; and this work happens on the *plane of understanding*, and not on the *activity plane.*

I published the second edition of this book a couple of years ago, but then I felt a dire need to elaborate certain points in a more detailed and simpler manner. So, I made a small revision to the content in a few places.

Hence, this third edition.

I hope you find it useful.

Choice Vs. Destiny

The debate of *choice vs. destiny* speaks of two contrasting opinions:

The *choice opinion* states that we do have free-will, therefore we do have choice over our decisions and activities.

The *destiny opinion* states that we do not have free-will because we are bound by destiny, therefore, we do not have any choice over our decisions and activities.

This debate gets settled when we realize that both these factors are a pair of opposites, and all the pair of opposites belong to a mysterious entity called *Maya*.

The term *Maya* implies a grand illusion that is devoid of intrinsic existence, yet which appears as a transactional phenomenon made up of forms, actions and cause-effect relationships.

The *Maya* makes us believe in the presence of objects which do not exist in reality.

The same *Maya* makes us take a *non-self object* as the *self*.

Consequently, we tend to think that the *self* is an individual personality which must necessarily be the subject of the phenomenal world.

This idea keeps us trapped in the ferocious cycle of life and death, and then we are left with no option but to face the sorrows and miseries of the phenomenal world.

The only way to overcome the *Maya* is to discover the *real self* who happens to be a formless existence, and who does not have any subjectivity vis-ā-vis the maya.

This discovery is called *self-realization* in spiritual parlance.

For the sake of argument though, one can say that between the two opinions of the *choice vs destiny* debate, the latter one has a more logical and a more comprehensive reasoning behind it.

Perhaps, you will agree to it after reading this book.

There is one more way to look at the duo of choice and destiny:

When we associate ourselves to the *plane of actions*, at that time we tend to think that we have a choice; but when we associate ourselves to the *plane of understanding*, at that time we tend to think that we are bound by destiny; and these two planes are separate operative grounds, therefore, the duo of choice and destiny can coexist, albeit at different levels. That way there can be harmony between the two.

However, the fact remains that whichever way you look at the duo, they still are the two sides of the *Maya*.

Preface

Power Of Words

A common view regarding the *methods of self-realization* is that *'words alone are not sufficient for the attainment of self-realization.'*

The supporters of this view claim that an *activity-based practice* is essential to attain the *self-realization.* Therefore, they tend to take recourse in rituals, yoga, austerities, external worship and devotional practices.

Those amongst them who are more vigorous and determined, adopt the path of Tantra (right-handed or left-handed methods).

Some others who are not bound by the prevailing concepts of sophistication tend to follow the *Aghora* path which involves practices like corpse worship and usage of addictive materials.

But the question is: Can the words alone become an instrument for self-realization?

The answer is: Yes, they can, most certainly, if we recognize the power of words.

What is this power of words?

Let us try to understand it the following way:

We carry out all our transactions using the words in our daily routine. If someone praises us, then we tend to feel happy, and if someone criticizes us, then we tend to feel annoyed.

If we take a closer look at this phenomenon, then we will understand that when somebody is either praising us or criticizing us, at that moment we do not get hit by a material. All that happens is: We get to hear the sound of the words uttered by the other person. When that sound reaches our ears, our mind starts analyzing it. After analyzing it, the mind starts interpreting it. If the mind gives us a positive interpretation, then we feel happy, and if the mind gives us a negative interpretation, then we feel annoyed.

The mind interprets the words using a relationship that exists between the words and their meanings.

The words tend to invoke the stored meanings in our mind.

The invoked meanings then create an understanding in our intellect, and this understanding enlightens us about the objects and the processes that the words were referring to.

This ability of the words to create understanding in us via their meanings is a result of the relationship that exists between the words and their meanings. This relationship is known as the power *of words* in philosophy.

The words of wisdom with their enlightening power give us a certain *understanding* of the existential reality.

When this understanding becomes clear and doubtless, then it is called *self-realization.*

Words do not require supplements of any activity-based practice to create an understanding in our intellect vis-a-vis the existential reality, because the existential reality remains ever present within us. Words are required only to make us aware of its true nature.

It is possible that listening to the words of wisdom for the first time may or may not make us realize the truth suddenly, but a repeated contemplation of them certainly has the capacity to make us realize the truth eventually.

This contemplation cannot be called as an activity-based practice in the usual sense, and it is only required for those who may not get the realization in the first listening.

Under the *spell of ignorance*, we tend to think that we are individual subjects with a body-mind complex, and that we possess a qualitative personal character; but the more we listen to the words of wisdom, the more our understanding grows about the nature of our *real self*.

If we continue to ponder over the words of wisdom then we eventually come to the realization that our *real self* is a formless existence.

This existence is unqualified in nature and it is *pure consciousness*.

On account of this realization, a transition of identification takes place. The realization vis-ā-vis our *real self* brings a great peace, and it opens the door of liberation for us.

On the path of knowledge, therefore, using the enlightening power of the words, great masters like Ashtavakra share the spiritual wisdom in a verbal form, and able seekers of truth like King Janaka, grasp it to attain *self-realization*.

Introduction

Goal Of Spirituality

The ultimate purpose of having spiritual wisdom is *attainment of eternal freedom* from suffering.

This eternal freedom from suffering is called *Moksha* or *liberation* in spiritual parlance.

We can attain *liberation* only when we - who take ourselves as the *individual selves* - will get liberated from the cycle of birth and death.

What is it that makes us think that we are the *individual selves*?

The spell of ignorance.

What kind of ignorance?

The notion that *I am an individual who is the doer/experiencer subject of the time-space phenomenon.*

Interestingly enough, this notion of *being an individual self* is only a concept of an ignorant intellect. The ignorant intellect makes us identify ourselves with an apparent individual persona. Yet, due to the effect of this identification, we tend to subject ourselves to the cycle of birth and death, and also to the subsequent suffering.

If we wish to attain liberation, then we will have to get rid of this notion that *I am an individual self.*

We will have to understand that our *real self* is an all-pervasive *being* that exists well before the ignorant notion comes into effect.

The all-pervasive *being* is a formless existence and it is un-qualitative in nature. It is an omnipresent reality that remains ever present as an independent existence.

This existence is *the only reality*; therefore, it remains devoid of all duality.

The task of *realizing the non-dual existence as our real self* is not as herculean as it may sound, because we are not required to convert ourselves into that existence physically or mentally. We are already *that*. We are only required to remove the doubts in our intellect about the fact that *we are that*.

This realization is not self-hypnotism; because the wisdom of *non-duality* comes from the revelations made by the sages who had realized this truth beyond doubt; and it is backed by an *evidence-based philosophical scrutiny*.

Chapter 1

Verse 1.1

King Janaka asked Sage Ashtavakra,
"How to gain knowledge? How does liberation happen?
How to have dispassion? Tell me this, O my Lord!"

Doubt: In spite of being a king, what made Janaka seek the knowledge of liberation? Why did he want to become dispassionate?

Answer: Janaka was a king, enveloped by riches and fame, but he had a pure mind and a sharp intellect. He realized the fallacies and limitations of the worldly pleasures that surrounded him.

He realized that all the pleasures are followed by great suffering, and all the objects in the world are impermanent.

He was not interested in momentary happiness, instead, he was looking for a measure to free himself from the suffering permanently.

Therefore, the search for everlasting peace, the search for eternal bliss, and the search for existential truth made him ask these questions.

Verse 1.2

Ashtavakra replied,
"If you want liberation, Son! Renounce the sensory pleasures as if like poison,
Worship forgiveness, politeness, compassion, contentment, truth, like nectar."

This is an interesting verse of the *Ashtavakra Gita*. On the face of it, this verse appears to be fairly simple in its meaning, and a lay person can also understand it; but it becomes interesting because none other than Ashtavakra is saying it. Why so?

Because as we move ahead, we will read Ashtavakra stating in many verses that for the truth to be realized a person neither needs to renounce a psychological trait nor does he need to acquire one. In other words, the realization of the existential truth does not depend upon the psychological inclinations of an individual person.

But why then, in this verse, Ashtavakra is asking Janaka to renounce sensory pleasures, and acquire forgiveness?

The answer is: Mirror cannot reflect light when it is covered by dust. The dust acts as an obstacle for its reflection. The presence of light does not depend upon the clarity of the mirror, but the reflection of it does depend upon the clarity of the mirror.

For the light to get reflected properly, *removal of the dust* is essential.

The presence of the formless existence does not depend on the qualities of an individual mind, but the reflection of its light does depend on the purity level of the mind.

Therefore, it is essential that the dust from the mind should be removed primarily. What does *dust* here refer to? Resentment, rudeness, cruelty, and greed.

To remove these obstacles, Ashtavakra prescribes the cultivation of qualities such as forgiveness, politeness, compassion, and contentment.

The word *truth* in this verse does not refer to a quality because the *ultimate truth* is not a quality in itself, but it is an existence. Hence, the *truth* cannot be acquired like other qualities.

By the word *truth*, Ashtavakra implies *commitment to the truth.*

Verse 1.3

"You are neither earth, nor water, nor fire, nor air, nor space,
For liberation, know yourself as the witness of all these."

The entire creation is made up of five basic elements: *Earth, Water, Fire, Air and Space.*

The bodies, minds and intellects of individuals are also made up of these elements.

Our *real self* is the witness of these elements, but under the spell of ignorance, we tend to believe that we ourselves are the bundle of body, mind, and intellect. In other words, we tend to attach our idea of *Self* to the *combination of body, mind and intellect.* Due to this attachment, we develop an idea of *ours being an individual self.*

Ashtavakra wants Janaka to give up this wrong idea. Instead, he wants Janaka to grow in his understanding about the *real self*; and realize that he does not belong to the world of five elements; on the contrary, he is a witness of these five elements.

What is the result of knowing ourselves as the witness? The next verse explains it.

Verse 1.4

"If you separate yourself from the body and rest in the *consciousness*,
Immediately you will be blissful, peaceful and free of all bondages."

Ashtavakra is asking Janaka to rest his *idea of self* in the *consciousness*, and not in the intellect.

There is a difference between *consciousness* and intellect. Intellect is a material layer whose mechanical function helps us acquire the dimensions and qualities of an object, whereas, consciousness is an existence that recognizes the acquired information by virtue of its conscious nature.

When our focus shifts from the intellect to the consciousness, we move closer to knowing ourselves as the *witness*.

If Janaka could do that, then he would find eternal bliss, everlasting peace, and he would be free of all bondages.

Doubt: Ashtavakra is asking Janaka to separate himself from the body; but, if the *real self* of Janaka is the physical body then he cannot separate himself from the physical body, and if Janaka is not the physical body then whom should he separate from it?

Answer: The physical body is a material body which is ever-changing. The body has changed substantially since our birth. However, the sense of *'I'* was there since our birth, and it is still there with us. So, our material body is ever changing but the sense of *'I'* is not changing. Hence, the material body cannot be the *real self*. Also, the subtle body cannot be the *real self*, because that is also a material body made of subtle materials; and that also is ever changing.

Doubt: Then whom Ashtavakra is asking to get separated from the body of Janaka?

Answer: In this verse, the word *separation* implies *getting rid of wrong idea*. The individual who was standing in front of Ashtavakra was having this wrong idea in his intellect that *I am this individual persona named Janaka*.

Ashtavakra is asking that individual to merely give up on that idea, because the idea that *I am an individual persona* arises from the idea that *I am an individual subject with an individual self*; and this idea is called *ignorance* in spirituality since it keeps us away from realizing our *real self* who is *witnessing consciousness*.

If the real self is not an individual body, then the attributes of an individual body do not apply to the real self. The next verse explains it.

Verse 1.5

"Neither you belong to any *caste*, nor to any *stage of life*, nor can be seen by the eyes,
You are unattached, formless, witness of the universe, hence, be blissful."

In ancient India, the society was divided into four types of *castes*, and the lifespan of a human being was divided into *four stages.*

The four types of *castes* were Priests, Warriors, Traders and Laborers. The four *stages of life* were Childhood, Student-hood, Married life and Monk-hood.

But, technically speaking, this socio-religious system would remain applicable to only that person who considered himself to be *a worldly person with an individual self.*

But, if he could transcend the *sense of being an individual self*, and realize himself as the *pure consciousness*, then for him, the barriers created by the socio-religious system would not remain applicable.

In this verse, Ashtavakra is asking Janaka to realize himself as the *unqualified existence*, and be free of all social and religious barriers.

Now, if someone is to transcend these barriers, and realize himself as the *formless self*, then is he required to do anything special?

Ashtavakra answers this in the next verse.

Verse 1.6

"The merit and demerit, happiness and sorrow are related to the mind and not to you, O Infinite!
You are neither the *doer* nor the *enjoyer*, you are eternally free."

Performance of a prescribed religious ritual, or righteous conduct in general, generates the merits.

Performance of a prohibited ritual, or a harmful activity in general, generates the demerits.

The merits and the demerits get stored on the material fabric of the mind in the form of impressions.

Technically speaking, the *mind* is one of the eighteen fabrics that make the subtle body; however, in this verse, Ashtavakra is referring to the entire subtle body as the *mind.*

When an individual dies, the subtle body gets separated from the gross body.

Then, depending on the cumulative dynamics of the merits and the demerits, the subtle body either travels to the heaven or to the hell, or it seeks another gross body on the earth to start a new earthly life to work out a new set of *destined karma.*

In each of these cases, it still remains bound by the laws of nature, and still remains subject to the experiences of pleasure and pain, due to the effect of *ignorance*; and also due to the fact that it can stay in those worlds for only a limited amount of time.

The course of heavenly life also comes to an end for the subtle body once it exhausts its merits during heavenly indulgences.

In short, no matter where the subtle body travels with an idea of *individual self*, its bondage continues, and subsequently suffering also continues.

This course of the subtle body, however, matters to the person whose *'I'* remains attached to the *mind.*

All the objects in the creation are following their course as per the destiny, but the ignorant mind makes one think that it is the *individual self who is the doer of activities as their subject.*

In other words, the ignorant mind creates an idea that the individual has a *choice* over the decision of doing or not doing.

Such an individual fails to understand that the so-called choice of his, is being guided by his destined karma, which is a result of the merits and demerits of his past lives; but, due to ignorance, he tends to think that he himself is the doer and enjoyer of the deeds done by his body.

Therefore, in the second sentence of this verse, Ashtavakra is asking Janaka to get rid of this *false idea* of *him being the doer/enjoyer subject.*

Verse 1.7

"You are the one, *seer* of all, eternally free,
Your bondage is that you see the *seer* as separate from yourself."

When we perceive material objects, we become the *seer*, and those objects become the *seen.*

The *seer* always has to be different from the *seen* objects.

Just as we can perceive other objects as the *seer*, we can perceive our physical body too as its *seer.* It means, the one who perceives the physical body is different from the body itself, yet we take the physical body as our *self* and get subjectively attached to it.

Same is the case with the psychological body which is also a material body made up of subtle materials.

Although, *us* as the *seer* are different from the physical and psychological bodies, still we end up taking the bodies as our *self.*

This is a phenomenal paradox. This paradox exists because the intellect has confusion about the real nature of our *self.* This confusion is called *ignorance* in spiritual parlance. Due to which, our idea of *'I'* gets attached to the body, and that makes our intellect think that we are the individual body. This individuality brings the bondage. Due to the bondage, we suffer.

Doubt: When we think of God, at that time, we can say that God is an object of our perception. Does it mean that God also becomes a *seen* object?

Answer: God is an eternal seer, and we can never think of God as an object of perception.

We can realize God only as our *real self*, through a subjective process of realization that takes place within the intellect. The eternal *seer*, in its entirety, can never become a *seen* object or an object of our objective thought-process.

Doubt: If God can never become an object of our objective-thought process, then how does knowledge work? Since knowledge remains bound by our objective-thought process.

Answer: Knowledge does not show us God objectively. Knowledge only removes *ignorance* about the nature of him. Once *ignorance* is removed, what remains is the real God: the *eternal seer* who is an omnipresent existence and who is pure consciousness by his very nature.

Doubt: But in the deep sleep, we do not perceive anything. Does it mean that during the deep sleep, the *seer* vanishes?

Answer: In the deep sleep also the *experience of relaxation* gets perceived and collected by the subject. That is the reason, when we wake up, we can ascertain our experience of the deep sleep by saying *I was sleeping very peacefully*.

Doubt: But then why can't we say so during the deep sleep when the experience remains there?

Answer: Because there is a difference between *experience* and *expression*.

Expression is the function of speech and mind. During the deep sleep, neither the speech works nor the mind. So, although the experience of relaxation remains there in the deep sleep, the expression of speech does not work there. We experience without expressing.

Doubt: We remain capable of breathing during the deep sleep. It means *Prana* (the air within our body) is the *seer*, because it remains active during the deep sleep.

Answer: No. *Prana* cannot be the seer because we can perceive it as an object of perception. So, it is a *seen* object and not the *seer*. Also, the air is an inert material, therefore it cannot have the ability to recognize experience. It needs the *power of consciousness* for its activity. That *consciousness* is the *eternal seer* - who can perceive the experience of the deep sleep.

Doubt: Then how can one know the *consciousness*?

Answer: We can realize it through separating the *'I'* from all the objects of perception. Which means we can only realize it through the process of knowledge that gets carried out subjectively within our intellect, and that helps us discover the real nature of the *seer*. Then we realize the fact that *the consciousness is our real self*.

Doubt: How to recognize this realization of the *real self*?

Answer: Broadly speaking, there are no tangible measures to evaluate this realization, but we can say that when the effects of the worldly objects stop causing sufferings for the *'I'*, then it can be taken as a sign of correct understanding required for *self-realization*, especially if it has come from the understanding of impersonal evidence such as spiritual scriptures.

Verse 1.8

"Stung by a great dark snake of false pride *I am the doer*;
By drinking the nectar of the belief - *I am not the doer*; be blissful."

Due to *ignorance*, a person believes that he is an individual subject, and he is the doer of activities. He believes that he is free to decide.

What he fails to realize is that his decision is getting caused by his destined karma.

The destined karma influences the intellect, the intellect then influences the mind, and the mind influences the body to act in a certain way.

So, it is the destined karma which works itself out through the body, mind and intellect. Body, mind and intellect are merely the instruments for the destined karma to work itself out.

There is no scope for an individual person consisting of body, mind and intellect to make decisions independent of his destined karma; but, due to *ignorance*, the mind makes us believe that we, as individual subjects, are the decision makers.

In this verse, Ashtavakra is asking Janaka to get rid of this false sense of doer-ship.

Once the sense of doer-ship vanishes, a great bliss comes. Mind drops obsessions, so also the worries, tensions and apprehensions of the future.

The sense of doer-ship comes with the idea of *I being an individual subject.* Ashtavakra, therefore, wants Janaka to get over the sense of individuality, which he expresses in the next verse.

Verse 1.9

"By the fire of conviction – *I am one pure consciousness*,
Having burned the deep ignorance, be free of grief and be blissful."

Grief is a condition of mind which occurs when an individual loses a dear thing. To get over all the grief, and to be permanently blissful, one needs to understand his true nature – *pure consciousness.*

When we realize ourselves as *pure consciousness*, we tend to become free of grief. The realization *'I am pure consciousness'* needs to be there with a certain degree of conviction.

Doubt: For this conviction to come, should we chant *I am pure consciousness*, like we chant a mantra?

Answer: Conviction does not come by mechanical repetition. Conviction comes when the doubts get removed. We need to focus on the meaning of the sentence *'I am pure consciousness'*. The more we grasp its meaning, the more we understand our true nature.

Doubt: Is there any difference between the *seer* and the *pure consciousness*?

Answer: The *seer* and the *pure consciousness* are the same.

If the *seer* would have been different from the *pure consciousness*, then the *seer* would become an inert object, and he would not have the ability to recognize experiences.

But we do have an element in us that always has the ability to recognize experiences. This element is a non-material reality, called *pure consciousness*. Hence, the *seer* and the *pure consciousness* are the same. When described in terms of witnessing, he is called *seer*, and when described in terms of knowing, he is called *consciousness.*

Verse 1.10

"Where this universe appears, like a snake appears on a rope,
Bliss, ultimate Bliss, that consciousness is you, move happily."

Sometimes, due to ignorance, a rope lying on the ground appears as if it is a snake. Similarly, due to ignorance, the forms of this world appear in the formless existence.

When we take ourselves as an individual form, we believe that we are part of the world of appearances, and forget our true nature which is the formless existence.

Doubt: Mistaking the appearance of a snake on a rope is possible because the form of a snake and the form of a rope are similar; but the qualified forms of the world cannot appear on an unqualified formless existence.

Answer: There is no rule as such that qualified entities cannot appear on top of an unqualified foundation. We perceive the sky as spherical and blue, but the sky does not possess shape or color.

Similarly, it is possible for the qualified world with shapes and forms to appear on top of an unqualified existence, given the fact that such an appearance is an illusion.

Verse 1.11

"One who thinks *freed*, is really free, one who thinks *bound* is really bound,
The phrase is true – *we become the way we think.*"

A person who thinks of freedom also tries to attain freedom. Eventually, with the correct understanding vis-a-vis the *real self*, he realizes that he is free by the very nature of his existence. He also realizes that he was never an individual form, but always the formless existence. It was only due to *ignorance* that he had mistaken himself as an individual form; and it had caused him great bondage.

On the other hand, a person – who takes false pride in his individuality – remains trapped in the bondage caused by the individuality.

Verse 1.12

"The real self is a witness, all-pervasive, complete, singular,
free, consciousness, inactive,
Unattached, devoid of craving, and peaceful. Due to ignorance,
he appears to be a worldly subject."

The *real self* – the *pure consciousness*, neither takes part in the activities of the world nor does he get touched by the objects of the world. He remains present as an eternal *seer*. He is the only reality; and therefore, is never required to perform actions to achieve objective results. Neither he needs to crave to fulfill object related desires.

But a person – who does not understand the self like this – mistakes himself to be a worldly person, and superimposes qualifications on top of his formless *real self*.

Doubt: If an individual is a composition of material elements, then he cannot perform the actions on his own, since material elements are inert. Therefore, we will have to believe that actions are performed by the *pure-consciousness*.

Answer: This doubt arises when we attribute reality to the actions; but actions are as illusory as the objects. In dream, we see a variety of actions; but they are as unreal as the phenomenon of the dream. The very nature of dream is illusory, including its objects and its actions.

Doubt: But if actions are unreal then how do they produce real effects? For example, when we touch the fire, we feel a sensation of heat.

Answer: The fire, the touch and the sensation are equally illusory. They get the sense of reality due to the presence of the *pure consciousness* in their background. The presence of that *pure consciousness* appears to be giving the sense of reality to the actions and to their effects, although the actions and the effects are as illusory as the forms they originate from.

Verse 1.13

"Contemplate on the non-dual, consciousness, *real self*,
By freeing yourself from the illusory *'I'*, feel the external as the internal."

The distinction such as *external and internal* comes with the sense of individuality. such a distinction cannot exist in the *real self* because he is non-dual *pure consciousness*. Things that appear external from the perspective of an individual, remain internal for the non-dual *consciousness*.

Doubt: To feel the external objects as the internal ones, should we expand the mind like a frog expands his abdomen?

Answer: Such an exercise will only prove to be futile.

The verses of Ashtavakra Gita should be interpreted in terms of understanding and not in terms of actions. '*To feel the external as the internal*' implies *realizing ourselves as the non-dual consciousness* so that the distinction between the external and the internal will not remain a real one.

Doubt: Does it mean that the individual will also vanish?

Answer: From the perspective of the other people, the individual will remain just the same, and the individual will continue to act the same as before. Only difference that will happen will be in his understanding about his *real self*. Earlier he would take himself as a material body but now he will realize himself as the non-dual *consciousness*.

Verse 1.14

"By the pride of the body, for a long time, you remained bound;
'*I am pure consciousness*', by this weapon, removing that pride, be blissful."

The sense of individuality gives rise to the sense 'I am the body.' We tend to take ourselves as a certain body with a certain form during the waking state; but during dream state, we tend to take ourselves as another body with another form. There is no real reason to believe that the waking state concepts are more real than the dream state concepts. More so, our waking state and dream state concepts about ourselves tend to disappear in the deep sleep. Therefore, our *real self* can neither be the waking state body nor can it be the dream state body.

Ashtavakra is asking Janaka to realize himself as the *pure consciousness* which remains present as the formless existence in all the three states. It remains present irrespective of the bodies that we assume ourselves to be during the waking, dreaming and deep sleep states.

Doubt: How can we say that the *pure consciousness* continues to be present in the deep sleep also?

Answer: The experience of the deep sleep gets recognized and stored due to the presence of the *pure consciousness* during the deep sleep.

The gross and the subtle bodies are inert objects made up of the material elements. They do not have the ability to recognize the experiences. The ability to recognize the experiences comes from the *pure consciousness* who is the *real sentient being*.

The experience of relaxation gets collected as an impression during the deep sleep. It means that someone must be recognizing that experience; for it to get collected as an impression.

The perceiver of that experience cannot be the mind because the mind does not function during the deep sleep. Neither can it be any other material element. It can only be the *pure consciousness* with his default *ability of recognition* who can perceive the experience during the deep sleep. He remains present in the deep sleep as the *real self* of the subject of deep sleep; just as he remains present as the *real self* of the subject of waking and dream state.

Doubt: Does it mean that the state of deep sleep is the same as the state of realization?

Answer: No, because the concept in the intellect of an ignorant person that *I am an individual self* remains intact during the deep sleep. This concept brings the *bondage*. Deep sleep, therefore, is not the same as *self-realization*.

More so, the waking, dreaming and deep sleep are the states caused by the transition of the mind. *Self-realization* is not a state caused by the transition of mind. *Self-realization* comes by getting rid of the concept of individual self, and by realizing the fact that the formless existence is our *real self*. Then the individual *'I'* wanes away, and the bondage caused by the individual *'I'* also wanes away.

Verse 1.15

"You are unattached, action-less, self-luminous and spotless,
Your bondage is that you practice meditation."

Our *real self* is unattached, action-less, self-luminous and spotless by the very nature of it. But when we take ourselves as *individual selves*, we try practices such as meditation to achieve *self-realization*. We tend to believe that if we tranquilize our mind through meditation then we will realize our *real self*. We tend to confuse the *stillness of the mind* with *self-realization*.

But, if we can just pay attention to our *real self*, then we will realize that our *real self* is peaceful by virtue of his existence. He never gets involved in the activities of the world; hence, he is neither required to perform any action nor any meditation. He is self-luminous in the sense that he is omnipresent. Also, there is no possibility that he will get affected or contaminated, because he is the only reality, and one without any second.

Doubt: Does it mean that meditation will not lead us to self-realization?

Answer: We may achieve temporary peace in meditation, but soon, the mind will get disturbed due to the forces of nature that are present inside and outside of the body.

The internal forces are karmic factors which an individual has to work out through actions. The external forces are environmental conditions like noise and temperature.

Even if we manage to calm the mind for some time and achieve complete stillness, that state will not be permanent, since these forces will disturb the mind.

More so, *self-realization* is not a state of mind.

Doubt: Then what is *self-realization*?

Answer: *Self-realization* implies *getting rid of the idea that 'I am an individual self who is the subject of phenomenal experiences'*

The idea of individuality vanishes when the doubts about our *real self* get removed.

The removal of doubts takes place in the following way:

First, we need to listen to the wisdom about the non-duality of the *real self*; given to us by the scriptures through verbal means. After that we have to pay more and more attention towards the *real self* as pointed by the scriptural wisdom.

There is a difference between *paying attention* and *doing the practice of meditation.* Attention does not require us to sit in a posture to artificially calm the mind. *Attention* implies *thinking about the real self with awareness.*

During meditation that takes place using a form, the thinking faculty subsides; while in *attention,* the thinking remains predominant. The more we think of the *real self*, the more it shines and unveils itself, since it is already present as our *being*.

Doubt: Does it mean that meditation is totally useless?

Answer: During our daily routine, our mind remains obsessed with many thoughts, and it wanders in all directions. This wandering of the mind proves to be an obstacle for paying attention towards the *real self*. Meditation is required only up to a point whereby this obstacle gets removed. After that, meditation should pave the way for the *attention*. For those who have a pure mind and sufficient grasping power, an explicit meditation is not required. They can realize the *real self* as soon as they get to hear about it. For those whose minds are not pure and wandering all the time, meditation can help up to a point of gaining some mental stability which is required to pay *attention*.

Verse 1.16

"This universe is pervaded by you, actually it is filled in you,
You are *pure consciousness*, do not become mean minded."

Doubt: Ashtavakra was giving this wisdom to Janaka - an individual who was standing in front of him. Then how come is he saying that *the whole universe is pervaded by you*? Does it mean that this verse is intended only to praise Janaka?

Answer: Words have two types of meanings: 1. Literal meaning 2. Implied meaning.

The Literal meaning of the word '*you*' is *the individual Janaka*, who was standing in front of Ashtavakra.

The Implied meaning of the word '*you*' is *pure consciousness*, which is non-dual and omnipresent existence.

In this verse, when Ashtavakra uses the word '*you*', he points at the implied meaning of the word.

In short, the whole world is pervaded by *pure consciousness*. Different shapes and dimensions of all the objects are mere superimpositions on the *pure consciousness*. Ashtavakra is asking Janaka to realize himself as the *pure consciousness*, and not to limit himself to an individual persona.

Once we realize ourselves as *pure consciousness*, the limitations and boundaries of individuality get transcended. Then it becomes easy to recognize that all the objects of the universe, including the individuals, are *the seen objects;* and our *real self* is *the seer.*

Doubt: An individual may be able to recognize that he is pervaded by the *pure consciousness*, but how can he recognize that all the other objects are also pervaded by it, since they are inert in nature, like rocks, clay, and ice?

Answer: Because those objects can be moved by external forces. If the *consciousness* would not have been present behind those objects, then their movement also would not have been possible. More so, then we would have been compelled to assume two powers: 1. The Power of Consciousness and 2. The Power of inert material; but inert material cannot be assumed to have power of its own, because it cannot retain its state for more than one moment.

That, which changes its states, cannot have its own power.

The *pure consciousness* doesn't change, as it never takes part in the affairs of the world. It only empowers the objects of the world with its presence.

Verse 1.17

"Devoid of expectation, perversion and dependence; sober in nature,
Unexcited, of unfathomable intelligence. Desire for pure consciousness only."

Doubt: If *pure consciousness* is present everywhere then why desire for *pure consciousness* alone and not for the worldly objects, since it is present in them also?

Answer: When an individual is at the initial stage of understanding, it is necessary that he should be encouraged to inquire into the nature of the subject. For this purpose, sometimes it becomes necessary to prevent him from thinking of other objects. A person – who is not longing for worldly objects – will be in a better position to carry out the subjective inquiry about the nature of his *real self*. His mind will stay introverted, and it will not become extroverted at the drop of a hat.

All spiritual masters, therefore, make the disciples enquire into the nature of the subject; and to promote their subjective enquiry, they advise them to give up the longing for worldly objects.

Verse 1.18

"Know the form as unreal and the formless as motionless;
By this wisdom, you will not come back to this world."

Doubt: Why not come back to the world?

Answer: An individual gets caught in the world through the ferocious cycle of birth and death. All individuals, without any exceptions, have to undergo pains, sufferings, sorrows, miseries, struggles and disappointments. The only way we can get rid of pains, sufferings, sorrows, and struggles, is by getting rid of the cycle of birth and death. For this purpose, it is required for us to understand that the forms of the objects are constantly changing, and therefore, they cannot be real. Only the *formless being* which is an unqualified existence remains unchanged for eternity. Hence, by knowing the formless existence as our *real self*, we are freed from our individual forms, and thereby we attain liberation.

Doubt: But for every pain there is a medicine. For every sorrow there is an object of entertainment, which removes the sorrow and brings happiness. And above all, every night, for a few hours of deep sleep, there is neither pain nor sorrow. So, when the world itself has many solutions to remove the pains and sorrows, then why to attain liberation which doesn't appear to be very exciting?

Answer: All the solutions present in the world, including the deep sleep, are temporary measures; but, if we have to end the sorrows totally and permanently, then the only way out is attainment of liberation, by getting rid of our sense of individuality, thereby getting rid of the cycle of birth and death.

Doubt: How to get rid of the sense of individuality?

Answer: By realizing that our *real self* is the *pure consciousness*, who is an eternal *seer* and an existence who remains unaffected by the developments of this world.

Verse 1.19

"Just like the mirror itself is there inside and outside of an image it holds,
The Lord is there inside and outside of this body."

The image in the mirror does not create a physical divide in the mirror. The image remains merely an appearance in the mirror. It means that the image in itself does not have any substance of its own, but it only appears as a virtual reality.

Similarly, there is only one existence – the *Lord* – inside and outside of our bodies. Bodies are virtual appearances.

Verse 1.20

"Just like space is there inside and outside of a pot,
Permanent, indivisible existence is there inside and outside of all beings."

Presence of a pot cannot create a physical divide in the space, therefore, the distinction such as '*inside space*' and '*outside space*' is not a real distinction. It is a fictitious distinction caused by an appearance of a virtual object – the pot.

Similarly, the eternal and indivisible existence is present inside and outside of all beings. The bodies are merely virtual objects which cannot divide the existence beneath them. That existence is formless and un-qualitative by its nature.

Chapter 2

Verse 2.1

King Janaka said,

"Oh! Spotless, peaceful, consciousness I am, beyond this creation.

Until this time, I was getting deluded by an infatuation only."

In the first chapter, sage Ashtavakra has given the highest wisdom in a nutshell. Listening to those words of Ashtavakra, Janaka became increasingly aware of his real self.

In the current chapter, Janaka is dwelling on his own realization. Janaka is amazed that he was always an unqualified existence, yet he mistook himself as an individual persona till now.

As he heard sage Ashtavakra narrate to him the nature of his real self, he got submerged in a state of ecstasy and felt relieved.

After listening to Ashtavakra, Janaka realized that he was always pure consciousness, thereby realizing that he was always spotless and peaceful by nature. He was always the *seer* and never was part of the *seen* objects.

Doubt: If the *real self* of Janaka was *pure consciousness* then what made him think that he was an individual?

Answer: Ignorance.

Doubt: What is its nature?

Answer: The word *Ignorance* implies *doubts vis-ā-vis the real self*. To dispel *ignorance*, all we are required to do is to remove doubts about the *real self*. Then we tend to realize the *real self* who always remains present with us.

Doubt: How can we say that the *real self* always remains present with us?

Answer: Because at any given point of time, we know that we exist. One cannot deny his own existence even for a moment. If somebody says 'I do not exist', then who is the one who says this? It means the presence of an ultimate existence cannot be denied. More so, there is always somebody whom we know as *'I'.*

Individual persona is the *literal meaning* of the *'I'.*

Pure consciousness is the *implied meaning* of the *'I'.*

The more the doubts about the *real self* vanish from our intellect, the more we travel from the *literal meaning* of the 'I' to the *implied meaning* of the 'I.' As a result, we become free of psychological sorrows forever and that is the goal of spirituality.

Doubt: Where do these doubts, the *ignorance*, reside?

Answer: In the intellect of an individual.

It remains, therefore, pertinent for us to remove these doubts by virtue of proper understanding of the *real self.* The most authentic sources of this wisdom are scriptures like the *Upanishads* and the *Ashtavakra Gita*, who in an unequivocal voice, make us aware of the *real self.*

Firstly, we need to listen to the words of scriptures. Then we have to contemplate on the meaning of those words to understand the subject they are pointing to. During this process we realize that we were never an individual persona, and that we were always an unqualified existence. It was only due to *ignorance* that we had mistaken ourselves as an individual persona for so long.

Doubt: If everybody's self is the unqualified existence, then for whom is this wisdom?

Answer: Wisdom is for those who believe that they are individuals due to the veil of *ignorance.*

Doubt: But they know that they exist.

Answer: Yes. One is certainly aware of one's existence. However, due to the spell of *ignorance* one does not know that an unqualified existence is his *real self*. When we take ourselves as qualified individuals of the qualified world, we suffer due to the limitations of individuality; but, when we realize ourselves as the unqualified existence, then the suffering comes to an end; because in that case we do not bind ourselves to the psychology of an individual, whom we previously identified with as the *Self*.

Verse 2.2

"As I illuminate this body and the world as well,
The whole world, therefore, is mine or else, nothing is mine."

Material bodies are made up of material of the world. Hence, technically speaking, we should perceive the material of our bodies just like we perceive the other material.

But, due to ignorance, we think that we are an individual body, and we tend to attach a lot more significance to the material of our bodies than that to an external material.

When we realize that we are not an object of perception but we are the perceiver, the seer, then we recognize our body in the same way as we recognize the other material of the world. Then we tend to realize that the one who perceives the body is the same as the one who perceives the world.

Verse 2.3

"Oh, along with the body, having abandoned the world too,
With some great skill, now God is seen."

Doubt: Janaka was standing in front of Ashtavakra. So how can he say that he has abandoned the world along with his body?

Answer: In this verse, abandoning implies 'separating the 'I' from the body and placing it in the witnessing consciousness.' This separation happens when we remove the mental bias that 'I am an individual persona'.

Doubt: Janaka is saying that 'God is seen.' Does it mean that God is different from Janaka?

Answer: 'God is seen' implies 'realizing God as his own self.' Janaka has realized himself as the pure consciousness. If God would have been different from the pure consciousness, then God would have been an inert material, and that is an absurd thought. So, God himself is pure consciousness who is the real self of all.

Doubt: If everyone can realize the pure consciousness as the real self then there must be a multitude of pure consciousnesses.

Answer: Definitely not, because the experience of deep sleep remains the same for everyone.

In deep sleep, when the mind is not active, the relaxation experienced by everyone is the same due to the perceived absence of the forms. It means the distinction of individuality comes only when the mind is active. Also, God is said to be infinite. If there would have been multiplicity of the existences, then they all would limit each other, and none of them would remain infinite.

Verse 2.4

"Just like the waves, the bubbles and the drops are not different from the water,
Similarly, the universe sprung out of me, is not different from me."

As materials, the waves, the bubbles and the drops are water only. Similarly, the world which has sprung out from the formless existence cannot be different from the existence itself. That formless existence is the real self. Materially, the effect cannot be different from the cause.

Doubt: But we do perceive the waves as waves, bubbles as bubbles and drops as drops. They have their own appearances with their size, shape, color, and other qualities.

Answer: Their qualities are appearance only. Their material, however, is the water. Appearance cannot exist independent of its material.

Doubt: Can the appearance be as real as its material?

Answer: No, because appearance can be changed. Size, shape and color of a clay pot can be changed. The clay, however, will remain the same, as far as this analogy is concerned.

Verse 2.5

"Cloth is thread only, when thought of properly,
Self-threaded only is this universe, likewise, when thought of properly."

A cloth is an integration of threads. As the material, cloth cannot be independent of threads. *Cloth* is just a name given to the appearance which emerges when the threads are tied together. Hence, the *cloth* in itself is not a separate entity.

Similarly, *Universe* is just a name given to the objects appearing in the formless existence, and this formless existence is the real self of all beings.

Verse 2.6

"Like sugar, made from the sugarcane juice, is filled with that only,
Similarly, the universe made from me, is filled with me only."

Doubt: The universe is said to be expanding. Does it mean that the real self also expands to fill the universe?

Answer: The universe and its expansion are merely in appearance. The real self is not a worldly material to expand or contract with the apparent universe. The real self is the foundational existence of the universe. That way, the universe is filled with the real self.

Verse 2.7

"Due to ignorance about the real self, the world appears. Not with the knowledge of the real self.
Due to ignorance about the rope, the snake appears. Not with the knowledge of the rope."

Sometimes when we see a rope in insufficient light, it appears as if there is a snake lying on the ground. Due to paucity of knowledge, we tend to perceive the rope as a snake; but with the proper knowledge of the rope, the perception of the snake disappears.

Similarly, due to ignorance of the real self, the world appears. With the knowledge of the real self, the world disappears.

Doubt: So, if we know our real self, will we stop seeing the world? Will we not experience anything after that?

Answer: Even after the realization of the real self, we will continue to see and experience the world as before, but the psychological effects of the worldly objects will reduce on our '*I*'.

As a result, we will be at peace with ourselves, and we will gradually lose our purpose in the world. In the absence of the purpose, we will not be born again as individuals and hence, we will attain the final emancipation.

Verse 2.8

"Light is my nature, I am not more than that,
When the universe appears, only then the feeling of '*I*' comes."

In this verse, the word *light* implies *pure consciousness*.

Our *being* is the all-pervasive pure consciousness. The distinction of '*I*', '*You*' and '*This*' comes when the universe appears in front of our senses, making us believe that we are an individual subject who is perceiving other objects which are separate from the *self*.

With the sense of individuality comes the feeling of an individual '*I*'.

Doubt: In the deep sleep, our senses do not work. Does it mean that in the deep sleep, the individual '*I*' vanishes?

Answer: In the deep sleep, the *feeling of being an individual 'I'* subsides, but the *concept of individuality* remains intact in the intellect, due to *ignorance*.

There is a difference between '*feeling of being an individual I*', and '*concept* of being an individual *I*'.

The *feeling of being an individual I* remains present during waking and dreaming states; but, the *concept of being an individual I* remains present during all the three states of waking, dreaming, and deep sleep.

In the waking and dreaming states, the *feeling of being an individual I* comes out from the *concept* of being an individual *I*.

In the deep sleep, since the feeling of individuality subsides temporarily, therefore only the concept of individuality remains present, of course, due to *ignorance*.

Verse 2.9

"Oh! Imaginary world appears in me due to ignorance,
Silver appears in pearl oyster, snake appears in rope or water
appears in bright sunshine, likewise."

Due to ignorance, when we limit our idea of *Self* to an *individual persona*, then the sense of separation between *me* and *rest of the world* comes; but once we realize that *the all-pervasive existence is our real self*, then we also tend to realize that the appearance of world becomes possible due to the foundation of our real self.

Verse 2.10

"Emanated from me, the world will dissolve in me only,
Just like a pot in the clay, a wave in the water, and an ornament in the gold."

The material cause of a pot is clay. The material cause of a wave is water. The material cause of an ornament is gold.

When the pot loses its dimensions, it gets dissolved into the clay. When the wave loses its dimensions, it gets dissolved into the water, and when an ornament loses its dimensions, it gets dissolved into the gold. Similarly, the material cause for the world is the real self. Therefore, when the world loses its dimensions, it gets dissolved into the real self.

Doubt: The world seems to be an eternal phenomenon. How can we say that the world loses its dimensions?

Answer: From an individual's point of view, the world loses its dimensions during the deep sleep. Deep sleep is a phenomenon during which an individual does not perceive the qualified world.

From the global point of view, the scriptural evidence tells us about the process of genesis and dissolution.

Verse 2.11

"Oh! I prostrate to me, whose destruction is not there,
From the creator to a blade of grass, even when the entire world gets destroyed, the *Self* remains."

Having realized an unqualified existence as his real self, king Janaka was in a state of ecstasy.

He realized that he was never an individual, and that he was always an unqualified existence. He realized that his true self is the imperishable existence alone.

Verse 2.12

"Oh! I prostrate to me, I am the one, in spite of being present in the body,
Neither goes nor comes, having filled the universe, just stays."

Doubt: If the self of Janaka is present in the body then how can he fill the entire universe?

Answer: Janaka has realized himself to be the all-pervasive formless existence. He has become aware that existence is as much present in other objects of the world as it is present in his body.

Verse 2.13

"Oh! I prostrate to me; here nobody is aware like me,
Not even being touched by an individual body, yet, by whom the universe is being held forever."

Doubt: How is it possible that without being touched by an individual body, the self is able to hold all the universe?

Answer: The real self is a formless existence; and the qualified universe is just a dream.

The objects of the universe only exist in appearance and not in substance. The real self remains present as the foundation for this appearance of objects.

A material body is just one object belonging to the *apparent* universe.

It is, therefore, perfectly possible that without being touched by its objects, the real self is able to hold the universe; just like the brain of a sleeping person holds the entire dream-world, without getting touched by it.

Verse 2.14

"Oh! I prostrate to me, who's nothing is, even a bit,
Or, who's everything is, that can be perceived by the mind and speech."

The phenomenal universe is a dream-like appearance which sustains due to the presence of the *real self*.

As a witness of the appearance, nothing belongs to the real self, or, as the background presence of the appearance, everything belongs to it.

Verse 2.15

"Knowledge, known and knower, this triad is not real,
The foundation, where it appears due to ignorance, is the spotless me."

The distinction of knowledge, known and knower is relevant from an individual's point of view; but, when we realize the all-pervasive existence as our real self, then the distinction of knowledge, known and knower vanishes.

Verse 2.16

"Oh, sorrow has its root in the duality, no other remedy for it,
This appearance is unreal, there is only one presence, which is the pure consciousness, which is me."

Doubt: If only one existence is there then from where the sense of duality arises?

Answer: The sense of duality arises in the intellect due to ignorance vis-ā-vis our *real self*. When the intellect develops an idea that *'myself is this individual person'* then the sense of duality arises.

Verse 2.17

"*I am pure consciousness only, due to ignorance I have assumed the portrait,*

Constant thinking of this kind, gets me established in the state of non-duality."

Constant contemplation of the *real self* removes the doubts in the intellect about our true nature. Then comes a time when the intellect does not doubt that the *real self* is the formless existence. As a result, one gets established in his original self, which is the non-dual existence.

Doubt: How does thinking remove the sense of duality?

Answer: The sense of duality comes from the misunderstanding about the real self. This misunderstanding is a non-material entity. Hence, it can be corrected only through proper and evidence-based thinking. Then, the non-dual existence can be realized as the real self.

Verse 2.18

"Oh! Universe situated in me, is actually not situated in me,

For me, there is neither bondage nor liberation, baseless illusion has subsided."

Spontaneous revelations, the joy of having understood the real self. A big sigh of relief!

Verse 2.19

"Along with the body, the world is nothing really; convinced like this,
Self is *pure consciousness*, in whom is this illusion possible."

The realization that the world is an illusory perception and not a real entity.

Doubt: Does it mean that the one who understands the real self will not perceive the world anymore?

Answer: He will still perceive the world, but without getting affected by it.

Verse 2.20

"The body, heaven and hell, bondage and liberation and fear likewise,
Imaginary only, what work is there for me, the pure consciousness."

Janaka realized that the bondage was an idea, and not a material in itself.

He realized that liberation is also not a material object either. The idea of bondage was removed by the proper understanding of the real self.

Since he does not see a purpose in the dream creation any longer, therefore, he does not see himself as a duty-bound individual.

Doubt: Does it mean that he will become inactive?

Answer: Certainly Not. The individual will still be seen as an active individual due to the remaining destined karma of that individual. However, it will be more of a role-playing on his part, as the affairs of the world would no longer be able to entice him.

Hence, he will not attach the flight of imagination to the activities done by his body.

Verse 2.21

"Oh! Even in the masses of people, duality is not seen by me,
As if it were a covered forest, where should I have affection?"

Having realized himself as the non-dual pure consciousness, Janaka's sense of duality has vanished. Along with it, he has also lost the sense of meaning in the world. Now life has become deserted as if it were a covered forest. Due to the loss of meaning, all of his attachments have also vanished.

Verse 2.22

"I am not the body nor the body is mine nor am I an individual, I am pure consciousness,
My only bondage was my craving to stay alive."

When we want to stay alive as an individual persona with the belief that we are one particular body, then that belief becomes the main cause of our bondage.

Janaka has realized himself as pure consciousness, so, his ideas such as *'my body'* have vanished.

Doubt: But even the knowledgeable person uses the terms like *'I', 'My body'* etc.

Answer: A self-realized person uses the terms *'I', 'My body'* etc. to carry out the routine transactions. It is more of a formality on his part than any substantial business.

Till the destiny of the present body does not get lived out completely, the body of the knowledgeable person will continue to function just like that of any other person. So, he will need it to carry out routine transactions; for that, the terms *'I'* or *'My body'* will be used by him, but without any real attachment to the body.

Verse 2.23

"Oh! Strange turbulences of the world suddenly arise,
In the infinite ocean of myself, with the rise of air of mind."

When the mind functions in the waking and dreaming state, an individual perceives the phenomenal world.

In the deep sleep when the mind remains dormant, the individual does not perceive the phenomenal world.

Therefore, in this verse, Janaka says that the world arises with the rise of the air of mind.

The real self is an all-pervasive formless existence. Therefore, the appearance of the perceived world takes place in the *infinite ocean of the real self.*

Doubt: The air of mind does not function in deep sleep. Does it mean that the deep sleep state is the same as the self-realization?

Answer: No. During the deep sleep state, an ignorant person keeps the notion of *his being an individual self* in his intellect.

The self-realization, on the other hand, dawns when this notion gets extinct.

Verse 2.24

"In the infinite ocean of myself, the air of mind subsides,
Due to the lack of fortune, the trader's ship gets destroyed."

Doubt: What is the *'air of mind'*? Is it the physical air flowing in the body?

Answer: The term *'air of mind'* in this verse implies *ignorance about the real self.* When ignorance gets dispelled by the correct understanding of the real self, the trader's ship gets destroyed.

Verse 2.25

"In the infinite ocean of myself, amazingly, many individual waves,
arise, collide, play and subside on their own."

Having realized himself as pure consciousness, Janaka is able to perceive his mind as a witness. He is able to perceive different waves of thoughts, ideas and emotions arising in his mind by staying independent of them. Hence, he is getting amazed by looking at the *play of mind* without getting involved in it.

Chapter 3

Verse 3.1

Ashtavakra said,

"Having principally realized the imperishable self,
How come your interest in earning money?"

Doubt: Does it mean that the self-realized person will not earn any money?

Answer: The self-realized person will earn as much money as is required to complete his remaining destined karma; however, he will not hanker after money thinking that the money will bring him eternal happiness.

Doubt: Why does a self-realized person need to complete his remaining destined karma?

Answer: Destined karma gets momentum prior to the birth of an individual; well before he realizes his real self. Hence, he will have to complete its course by practically working it out in the material world. Till then, his body will remain functional in the world.

There are three types of karma:

1. *Stock karma* (Sanskrit word - *'Sanchita'*).
2. Destined Karma (Sanskrit word - 'Prarabdha')
3. Newly generated karma (Sanskrit word - 'Aagami')

The *stock karma* is the whole aggregate of karmic impressions that have got stored on our subtle body due to our actions in the past.

The *destined karma* is a small portion of the *stock karma.* It gets activated prior to our birth, and it determines the lifeform, lifespan and experiences for us, for a particular life.

The *newly generated karma* are the karmic impressions which get newly incurred due to the intentional actions performed by us under the spell of ignorance.

These newly generated karmic impressions can become a part of our ongoing *destined karma;* or they can become part of the *stock karma*, and become the part of destined karma for a future life.

The *stock karma* remains dormant while the *destined karma* gets worked out in one particular lifetime. The *destined karma* needs to complete its course by getting worked out through the body.

So, in the eyes of others, the body of a self-realized person will still function till his remaining destined karma gets worked out fully.

The self-realized person understands it; therefore, he will earn money due to the force of the destined karma, but his mind will not have an extra desire to earn pleasures of the world through accumulating wealth.

Verse 3.2

"Due to ignorance about the real self, Oh, interest in illusory objects of pleasure.
Just like due to ignorance about a pearl oyster, infatuation prevails, in an illusory silver."

In the moonlight, a pearl oyster gets mistaken as a piece of silver. This perceptible silver attracts the observer, and develops an infatuation in his mind for it.

When we take ourselves as the individual selves, we get attracted towards the objects of the world, thinking that those objects will give us pleasure. This kind of thinking develops an infatuation in our mind for those objects.

The pleasures those objects bring to us, however, remain momentary, eventually they turn into sorrow.

At the root of it, remains our incorrect idea about ourselves that our self is an individual persona who is a subject of worldly experiences.

Verse 3.3

"Where this universe surfaces like waves in the ocean,
Having known it as *'I am that'*, why do you run like a poor person?"

The foundation of this apparent universe is an all-pervasive existence. The apparent universe surfaces in it, so to speak, like the waves surface in an ocean. Having known that existence as our real self, why should we run as if we are missing something? What remains to be sought?

In this verse, a person who seeks happiness outside of his real self, has been called a *'poor person'*.

Verse 3.4

"Having heard also that *'I am the beautiful pure consciousness'*,
One who is extremely attached to sexual pleasures, becomes malicious."

Desires create attachments, and attachments cause bondage.

Having heard about the real self, we should engage ourselves in the contemplation of it, instead of getting swayed by the desires.

Doubt: Does it mean that Ashtavakra is prescribing strict celibacy as a pre-condition to gain knowledge?

Answer: In the above verse, the word *'extremely'* is important. Getting swayed *extremely* by any desire causes bondage, however, indulgence caused by the force of destined karma will not cause bondage.

Doubt: How to distinguish between indulgence caused by the force of destined karma and that caused by an extreme desire?

Answer: An indulgence which makes us find extraordinary ways for its fulfillment can be taken as the one caused by an extreme desire; and it is bound to make us malicious.

Verse 3.5

"The *Self is in all the beings, and all the beings are in the self*,
The sage who knows it, surprisingly, still follows attachments."

Doubt: How is it possible that he will still follow attachments?

Answer: There can be two reasons:

First one is: *Destined karma.*

Due to the destined karma, he might continue to have certain likes and dislikes, till his body remains functional.

Second reason is: The difference between intellectual knowledge and actual realization.

He might have the knowledge that has remained restricted to the intellectual level, without it getting converted into a deeper realization.

When the mind is not pure enough, and when the earnestness for liberation is not strong enough, the knowledge may remain restricted to intellectual level, and would not penetrate further to become a deeper realization.

Verse 3.6

"Having loyalty in the ultimate non-duality, also knowing clearly about liberation,
Yet helpless, gets driven by desires due to past habits."

An individual's habits arise from his destined karma. They compel him to act in a certain way in order to fulfill his desires. In a way, he remains helpless before the force of his destined karma.

Doubt: Then what is the outcome of gaining knowledge?

Answer: The knowledge leads a person to the realization of his *real self*, thereby, making him understand that he was never the subject of karma; because the *real self* is a formless and un-qualitative existence who is devoid of all subjectivity vis-a-vis the world.

This realization liberates him from the cycle of birth and death, thereby ending his sorrows forever.

Verse 3.7

"When aroused, an enemy of knowledge, for the very weak also,
Surprising to get desirous, even when nearing his end."

In this verse, the term *enemy of knowledge* implies *desires*.

It has been seen that even a physically weak person, when nearing his end time also, gets driven by physical desires. This is very surprising; but it happens due to his *ignorance* about the nature of his *real self*.

Verse 3.8

"For the dispassionate, and the discriminatory between the permanent and the temporary things,
Surprising is the fear of liberation in him who is desirous of liberation."

The common misunderstanding about fear is that we fear the things which are unknown to us, but actually fear does not come from unknown things. Fear comes from the anticipation of loss of known things.

In the case of liberation also, the liberation-seeker does not fear liberation, but he may fear losing his present identity, the individuality.

This fear is totally unnecessary because liberation does not cause an immediate destruction of the personality. Liberation happens when the seeker gets rid of the doubts in his intellect about the fact that *our real self is a formless existence.*

These doubts are not material substances; therefore, their removal does not cause a material change in the personality. It causes the removal of subjectivity, thereby, reduction of psychological effects on the *Self.*

Verse 3.9

"The courageous person, whether pleased or pained, always,
Sees the self alone, doesn't get excited or angry."

The term courageous person in this verse implies an enlightened person.

He recognizes that the all-pervasive existence is his real self, therefore he realizes the difference between the being and the mind.

He does not get affected due to pleasures or pains. Hence, he has been termed as the courageous one.

Verse 3.10

"Sees his own functional body in the same way as any other body,
In praise and criticism also, how can he get excited."

An enlightened person does not remain bound by the worldly concepts of pride and prestige. Hence, he remains indifferent to praise and criticism.

Verse 3.11

"Seeing this world as merely an illusion, the *awe-less*,
Even as death nears him, how can the courageous get miserable."

Fear of death remains as long as the sense of *I being an individual self* remains.

We fear death because we think that *death will finish our existence*; and everyone wants to continue to exist.

However, the enlightened one realizes that his real self is an all-pervasive, indivisible, omnipresent existence; and this existence can never get destroyed because it is the only reality.

On account of this assurance that he gets from his very *being*, he does not become miserable even when nearing his death.

Verse 3.12

"Aloof is whose mind, the great soul, even in despair,
Such a self-satisfied person's comparison is there with whom."

Comparison can only be done between similar things.

The eternal, indivisible, non-dual existence, however, is one without any second.

The one who realizes this existence as his real self, cannot be compared with any other ignorant person who takes himself as *an individual personality with an individual person-hood.*

Verse 3.13

"By the very nature, one who knows that *this scene is nothing*,

'This is worthy of acquisition or this is worthy of abandonment',
what should he see like this."

The enlightened person does not take the world as a real phenomenon. Therefore, he does not tend to pick and choose one aspect of it over another.

Verse 3.14
"For him who has given up the passions, free of duality and without hopes,
Indulgence coming incidentally, is neither for pleasure nor for sorrow."

The root of psychological entities such as passion and hope, is the desire for happiness.

The enlightened person who remains blissful by nature, does not crave for – or refute – the indulgences coming his way on their own.

Chapter 4

Verse 4.1

Ashtavakra said,

"The courageous enlightened person's enjoyment of worldly pleasures,

Not the same as that of other ignorant worldly-minded people."

The difference between the enjoyments of an enlightened one and those of other people, is the *attachment.*

The enlightened one enjoys the pleasures coming to him without getting attached to them.

The worldly-minded people enjoy the pleasures by getting attached to them; and the attachment eventually causes suffering to them.

Verse 4.2

"Where all the deities, including *Indra*, want to be situated,

Oh! having situated there the enlightened person does not get excited."

In Hindu mythology, *Indra* is the king of all deities residing in heaven.

Knowing the fallacies of the pleasures of heavenly enjoyments, even Indra desires to take birth on earth to seek the knowledge of liberation.

Having got such a precious knowledge already, the enlightened person does not get excited, as his mind remains subsided due to the subliminal effects of the knowledge.

Verse 4.3

"Of the wise one, no touch internally with the merits and the demerits,

Of the sky, no touch with the smoke; although seen like that."

Just like the sky does not get physically affected by the touch of the smoke in it, the enlightened one does not get affected by the touch of the merits and demerits stored in his subtle body.

The subtle body is also a material body that is made up of subtle elements, which host the karma formed by the past activities.

The wise one who realizes himself as pure consciousness, does not tend to identify himself with the subtle body, although seen like that from outside.

Verse 4.4

"Self is all this, known by the great soul,

Impulsively behaving, who is capable of condemning him?"

Sometimes the body of an enlightened person may behave impulsively due to the force of destined karma, and he may invite condemnation by the other people.

The *ignorance* and the sense of individuality, however, do not remain effective in his intellect. Therefore, due to the lack of subjectivity, there is no one in there to suffer the condemnation.

In a way, the world remains incapable of condemning him.

Verse 4.5

"From the ruler of the world to a blade of grass, amongst the four kinds of beings,
Only a wise one remains capable enough of dropping *willingness and unwillingness*."

All the living beings can be divided into four categories based on how they come out during the birth:
Mammals-who come out from the womb.
Oviparous-who come out from the egg.
Species who come out from the earth; e.g., plants.
Species who come out from the sweat/fermentation.
Among these four types of creatures, only an enlightened person remains capable of dropping his *willingness* and *unwillingness*, since he does not take the world - and his mind too - to be real entities. He remains aware that the objects, as well as his mind, are parts of the apparent phenomena and not the realities.

Verse 4.6

"Non-duality of the self with the Lord, some rare person knows,
Whatever he thinks he does, no fear for him anywhere."

Since an enlightened person realizes his real self to be the imperishable and indivisible existence, he always remains united with the *Lord* - the pure existence.
Therefore, he does not fear anywhere.

Chapter 5

Verse 5.1

Ashtavakra Said,

"You are not attached, only pure, then what do you want to renounce?

By dissolving the combination like this, dissolve, move freely."

We were, we are and we will always be *pure consciousness*. We were never - and will never be - the combination of materials that is an individual body. Therefore, there is no scope for a physical renunciation.

Doubt: Then what should be dissolved?

Answer: In this verse, the word dissolution implies the loss of subjectivity due to enlightenment.

Verse 5.2

"Universe arises in you, like bubbles in the ocean,

Having known one real self like this, dissolve, move freely."

Ashtavakra is asking Janaka to dissolve his mind, meaning Janaka is expected to give up his sense of individuality which prevailed earlier, due to ignorance.

Verse 5.3

"Perceived, yet, due to unreality of it, the universe is not there in pure you,

Manifested like a snake in a rope. Dissolve, move freely."

In poor lighting conditions, a rope lying on the ground is mistakenly perceived as a snake. The snake remains there as an appearance only and not as a reality.

Similarly, the universe is there as an appearance but not as a reality.

Doubt: But as long as the snake is being perceived, why would it be not taken as a reality for that much period of time?

Answer: The objects of perception do not automatically become reality. Reality has to be permanent. The perception of the snake gets crushed with the knowledge of the rope.

Just like the snake in the example, the universe too is an appearance that is temporary, changing and subject to destruction. Hence, it cannot be taken as a reality.

Doubt: But the appearance of the snake can also cause a discontinuity in the knowledge of the rope?

Answer: No. When we understand a certain fact with evidence, then no kind of appearance can change our conviction.

This conviction – knowledge without doubts – becomes realization.

Verse 5.4

"Same in sorrow and happiness, complete, same in hope and despair,
Same in life and death, know like this; dissolve, move freely."

Ashtavakra is telling Janaka that his true nature is pure consciousness. It does not get affected by the dualities of the world. These dualities can be: sorrow/happiness, hope/despair, and birth/death of an individual body.

Chapter 6

Verse 6.1

Janaka said,

"I am like the infinite sky, the world is like a pot,
This is knowledge, hence, neither abandonment of this world,
nor acquisition of it, nor dissolution."

Just like the sky is there inside, outside and within a pot, the real self – the formless existence – is there inside, outside and within all the objects of the universe.

With this realization, nothing remains to be acquired, renounced or dissolved. Mere understanding of the real self is sufficient for self-realization. The more we understand the real self, the more our ideas of the *Do's and Don'ts* get reduced. The mind subsides further.

We tend to get over the ideas of acquisition, renunciation or physical dissolution.

Verse 6.2

"I am like an infinite ocean, the world is like a wave,
This is knowledge, hence, neither abandonment of this world,
nor acquisition of it, nor dissolution."

In this verse, Janaka is using a different simile.

Just like the ocean itself is there inside, outside and within the form of a wave; the formless existence is there inside, outside and within the form of the world.

Having understood that existence as the real self, nothing remains to be acquired, renounced or dissolved.

Verse 6.3

"I am like a pearl oyster, the imaginary universe is like a silver,
This is knowledge, hence, neither abandonment of this world,
nor acquisition of it, nor dissolution."

The simile of *pearl oyster and silver* used in this verse is different from the two similes used in the earlier two verses.
The similes in the earlier two verses recognize the universe as some sort of phenomenon, but the simile of *pearl oyster and silver* does not ascribe even an iota of reality to the phenomenal universe.
Just like the silver appearing in the pearl oyster is completely imaginary, the universe appearing in the real self is also completely imaginary.
With this realization, nothing remains to be acquired, renounced or dissolved.

Verse 6.4

"I am in all beings and all beings are in me,
This is knowledge, hence, neither abandonment of this world,
nor acquiring, nor dissolution."

'Since myself is the foundation of the apparent universe, I am inside all beings and all beings are in me'; with this realization, nothing remains to be acquired, renounced or dissolved.

Chapter 7

Verse 7.1

Janaka said,

"In my infinite ocean, a ship of the universe dwells here and there,
By its own inner wind; I have no intolerance towards it."

Since an ocean is far greater than a ship dwelling in it, therefore it doesn't get affected by the movement of the ship.

Similarly, since Janaka has realized that *he is the formless existence that is like an ocean, and the universe is like a ship dwelling in it;* he is least affected by the developments in the universe.

Hence, he is not averse to any particular development in the universe, and has no prejudice in his mind.

In the absence of prejudice, he is able to tolerate all the developments in the world without an iota of intolerance towards them.

Verse 7.2

"In my infinite ocean, this wave of the world on its own,
Whether it rises or sets, neither gains nor loses for me."

The amplitude of an ocean does not get affected by the arousal or merging of an individual wave.

Having known himself to be the formless existence, Janaka is no longer attached to the qualified forms of the world, and is not bothered about the creation or destruction of them.

Verse 7.3
"In my infinite ocean, imagination called a universe;
Extremely peaceful, formless, only this is how I stay."

All-pervasive unqualified existence is the reality, and the universe is imaginary. With this understanding, Janaka has become peaceful, and therefore, he stays as he is, without getting affected by the imaginary universe.

Verse 7.4
"Neither self is in the feelings nor are feelings in an infinite spotless self,
Hence, unattached, craving-less, peaceful, this is how I stay."

Since the all-pervasive existence is unqualified, there do not exist feelings or emotions in it, as they do in the mind.
Having understood that existence as the real self, Janaka has lost his cravings for worldly objects, and has become peaceful; and stays as he is.

Verse 7.5
"Oh! I am pure consciousness only, the world is like an optical illusion,
Therefore, *how* and *where* do I hold the concept such as *acquisition* or *renunciation*."

The concepts of acquisition or renouncing can only be there as long as we take the worldly objects as realities; but the moment we realize that the objects are illusory, and they exist only in appearance and not as a reality, the concepts such as *acquisition* or *renunciation* become irrelevant.

Chapter 8

Verse 8.1

Ashtavakra said,

"Bondage comes when the mind wants something, grieves for something,

Grabs or leaves something, gets pleased or annoyed with something."

The tendencies of want, grief, grabbing or leaving, getting pleased or annoyed, are the tendencies of the mind.

These will remain strong as long as the sense of reality in worldly objects remains strong.

The sense of reality in worldly objects remains strong due to the effect of ignorance.

Ignorance causes bondage and the subsequent suffering.

Verse 8.2

"Liberation comes when the mind neither wants something, nor grieves for something;

Nor does it grab something nor leave something; neither does it get pleased nor annoyed with something."

As the ignorance diminishes, the sense of reality in the worldly forms also diminishes. Hence, the tendencies of want, grief, grabbing or leaving, getting pleased or annoyed, also tend to get diminished. Along with them, the subjectivity also gets diminished. This is liberation.

Verse 8.3

"Bondage comes when the mind remains attached to some perspective,
Liberation comes when the mind becomes detached with all the perspectives."

Just like attachment can be there for worldly objects, it can be there for the perspectives formed by our intellect regarding the affairs of the world.

These perspectives lead us to form certain opinions about those affairs. This intellectual attachment to the perspectives and opinions, can actually be much stronger than the attachment for the gross objects.

Hence, it is equally, or even more, important to get rid of the attachment for perspectives; and not keep any preconditioning in the mind vis-a-vis them. The attachment towards perspectives causes greater bondage and absence of it brings liberation.

Doubt: But is it not the philosophical perspective that liberates us?

Answer: Yes, the philosophical perspective of non-dualism certainly brings liberation, but then it gets dropped on its own once it does its job.

Afterwards, the enlightened person need not carry it in the form of a point of view.

Verse 8.4

"When the *'I'* does *not* prevail, then liberation; when the *'I'* does prevail then bondage,
Knowing this, do not take or leave anything with any expectation."

The 'I' is nothing but a concept of our intellect. This concept binds us to a particular individual persona which we take as our *self*.

This concept stays in the intellect of individuals, and it has nothing to do with the existential reality as such.

The concept of *individual 'I'* is the most basic form of ignorance, and it is the greatest cause of bondage.

The removal of it – by means of knowledge – brings liberation.

Chapter 9

Verse 9.1

Ashtavakra said,

'Did it' and *'Not did it'* – when has this dual subsided, and for whom?

Knowing this, renounce the world through withdrawal, be *non-ritualistic.*"

The one who considers himself as an individual self takes himself to be a duty-bound person. He sees a purpose in the phenomenal world and is required to be active all the time. His mind always dwells on either the past events or on the future developments. He always sees some target to be reached, some goal to be accomplished, and some objective to be fulfilled.

Therefore, he takes the path of rituals, which involves a lot of activities.

He, however, finds that even before he accomplishes his first task, the next one is already ready, waiting for him. This way, he gets entangled in the activities.

As long as we take the world as a real phenomenon, we will continue to see purpose in it, and we will continue to believe that we have an unfinished business in it.

This sense of purpose leads us to remain trapped in the cycle of birth and death. The only way to get rid of this vicious cycle, and to attain liberation thereby, is to withdraw ourselves from the illusory purposes, illusory objectives, and illusory activities of the world, and try to understand our real nature which is the pure consciousness.

This withdrawal should not be a physical withdrawal, but it should occur in terms of understanding.

Verse 9.2

"Of some rare blessed person's, by observing the affairs of other people,
Desire for living, enjoying and knowing subsides."

A rare blessed person is he, who has a pure mind and sharp intellect. He observes the activities and life of other people along with his own experience of the world, and understands the fallacies of worldly desires.

All the people who engage themselves in worldly activities, and chase desires, ultimately get disappointed to find that the world is duel in its nature and it offers as much, or more, sorrow than it offers happiness. It always offers little pleasure with a great deal of suffering.

More so, the affairs of the world are full of contradictions and irony. A person with a pure mind and sharp intellect, ponders over this, withdraws himself intelligently, and subsides his mind with the knowledge of his *real self*.

Verse 9.3

"Impermanent is all this, contaminated by three kinds of pains;
Tasteless, condemnable, worthy of abandonment, knowing this, he subsides."

The three kinds of pain are: 1. Pain caused by natural calamities. 2. Pain caused by physical and psychological problems. 3. Pain caused by other creatures.

Everything in the world is impermanent including objects, relationships, emotions, and feelings. If we remain attached in any way to this ever-changing world, then we cannot escape the suffering.

Also, the worldly objects in themselves are not the source of pleasures. The objects only happen to be the occasional cause for us to enjoy the pleasures already present in our mind. The source of happiness is within us, and not outside. Hence, the objects in themselves are tasteless and not worthy of the chase.

Having realized it, the mind of the enlightened person subsides.

Verse 9.4

"When is the time or the stage when the pair of opposites do not trouble men?
Ignoring them, who remains content, attains the realization."

The world essentially offers a bunch of opposites, and it has inherent contradictions in it.

If we give even an iota of importance to one part of it, then we will have to accept the whole package of it, with its dualities, contradictions, sorrows and sufferings.

The only way out is to ignore it as a whole and remain content in the understanding of the real nature of our real self.

The person who manages to do so, attains the truth.

Verse 9.5

"Variety of opinions of great saints, monks and yogis,
Looking at those, gradually withdrawing from them, which human being is there who will not become quiet."

Numerous philosophies, paths, approaches, practices proclaim that truth can be realized only if you go by their way.

The real self, however, gets realized when the mind subsides with the realization that the real self is a formless existence that does not have any subjectivity vis-a-vis the world.

Those who only talk philosophy often get caught into the jugglery of words, and they remain away from the realization.

Those who take the path of some practice like external worship, get caught in some kind of show-off, and they too remain away from the realization.

An ordinary person gets confused by the variety of paths and theories, and that leads him to become quiet vis-a-vis the spiritual matters.

Verse 9.6

"Makes one aware about pure consciousness; is he not a Guru?
By giving the vision of detachment and indifference, who
protects others from the world."

The one who makes us realize our real self - the pure consciousness, by giving us the wisdom of detachment, and teaches us to remain indifferent in all circumstances, is the real guru. He protects us from the sorrows and miseries of the world by making us realize our real self.

Verse 9.7

"See the creation of five elements as the five elements only,
realistically,
At that very same moment you will be free of bondage and will
get situated in your real self."

Different forms of the world are nothing but different compositions of the five elements. Hence, instead of getting caught in the delusive forms, if we understand their substance -

the five elements, then we will be able to detach ourselves from them, and we will be able to remain indifferent towards them, which will eventually lead us to the realization of our real self.

Verse 9.8

"Desires are the world; get rid of all of them,
That is renounced by renouncing desires. Afterwards, let the position be just like that."

Desires make us to chase worldly objects, and in the process, we get attached to the forms of the world. This attachment becomes bondage. It becomes a barrier in the way of arriving at the truth. Hence, Ashtavakra is asking Janaka to renounce desires, and clear the obstructions. That will help him subside the mind. Afterwards, he will remain as an onlooker who will see the game of destiny without the need for personal intervention.

Chapter 10

Verse 10.1

Ashtavakra said,

"By renouncing the enemy - lust; and the disaster - wealth;
Rituals too, the cause of both; see them as unimportant everywhere."

Rituals are performed to gain wealth.

Wealth is gained to satisfy the lust.

Ashtavakra is asking Janaka to renounce all three - the rituals, the wealth and the lust - in order to have contentment.

Janaka will be able to renounce them if he does not see them as important. Therefore, Ashtavakra is asking Janaka to see them as unimportant.

Verse 10.2

"Like an illusory dream of three or five days,
Look at a friend, land, wealth, palace, woman and inheritance."

Everything in the world has a limited lifespan, including our association and relationships with friends, land, wealth, palace, woman and inheritance.

This is one way of reducing the attachments that we may have towards these entities; thereby creating the possibility of paying more attention towards our *real self*.

Verse 10.3

"Where there is lust, know that there is world,
By taking refuge in great renunciation, give up lust; become blissful."

When we take the objects of the world as realities, we tend to develop lust for them, and we tend to find a purpose with them.

This sense of reality and the sense of purpose create attachment in us by making us believe that *we are individual subjects who must necessarily depend on external objects for happiness.*

Ashtavakra cautions that where there is lust, there is world, and where there is world, there is sorrow.

The only way out is to take refuge in renunciation, and thereby giving up the lust.

Doubt: Does the detachment imply sitting in a quiet corner or under some tree, without doing any activity?

Answer: The real detachment comes from the correct understanding. Detachment is a mental quality.

As long as the body remains functional, an individual surely does some activity due to the force of destined karma.

If he, however, has a correct understanding of his real self – the pure consciousness – then the actions performed by the body do not create attachment in him, and they do not cause him any further bondage.

Verse 10.4

"Craving is bondage, and its end is called freedom,
Only by non-attachment to the world, satisfaction is gained, again and again."

Craving for worldly objects creates psychological attachments, which reinforce the bondage.

When the craving is over, the attachments also subside.

Attachments make us poor in the sense that they cause us to lose our morale, and they keep us bound to the world, making us miserable, time and again.

On the other hand, non-attachment lifts our morale, and it keeps us satisfied within ourselves. Real satisfaction comes not through the worldly pleasures but through the self-contentment because our *real self* – the formless existence – is complete in itself.

Verse 10.5

"You are the one, *pure consciousness*; the universe is inert and unreal,
Even ignorance is nothing, then why is there your desire for information?"

Our real self is pure consciousness and it is the only reality; while the universe is inert, and it is an illusory phenomenon.

Even *ignorance* is nothing in the sense that it is a non-material entity.

The term ignorance implies the doubts that prevail in our intellect about the nature of our real self.

Having known it that way, what more remains to be known? Nothing.

The *desire for information* is also a desire.

The *desire to know* remains as long as we take ourselves as individual subjects, and think that our *being* is not complete in itself.

With the realization of the *real self*, the mind subsides, and with it, the *desire to know* also reduces.

Verse 10.6

"Kingdom, sons, women, bodies, pleasures also,

Even if you remain attached to them birth after birth, still they perish."

Kingdom, sons, women, material body and pleasures; these things are ever changing, and ultimately, they perish.

Things do not become permanent just because we are attached to them.

One day, all those things perish, and if we remain attached to them, then we become sorrowful.

Verse 10.7

"Enough; *money*, *desire* and *meritorious deeds* also,
From these, peace never came to the mind in the jungle of this world."

Money, desires and merits cannot bring us permanent peace because of the objective dependency involved in them.

In this verse, Ashtavakra calls the world *a jungle* because the ignorant mind trapped in it never finds a way out of it; as long as the effect of ignorance prevails.

The ignorance about the real self is the darkness of this jungle.

Verse 10.8

"For how many births you have done deeds through the body, mind and speech,
They gave you sorrow and struggle; withdraw from them at least now."

Ashtavakra is trying to broaden the vision of Janaka.

Usually, our perspective of our life remains confined to our present condition, including present pleasures and present sorrows.

We ignore the fact that we have been in the cycle of birth, death, and miseries for a countless period of time.

Usually, we remain short-sighted, and therefore we only look for temporary solutions, and thereby, continue to carry the root cause of sorrows with us - *the ignorance.*

Hence, it is pertinent for us to broaden our vision, and have a holistic approach, if we wish to get rid of the sorrows forever.

It requires us reminding ourselves that we have been doing the rounds of birth and death repeatedly, only to have sorrows and miseries. We have had all experiences of the world, including that of heaven, hell and the mortal world multiple times.

This kind of holistic thinking leads us to find a permanent solution to the problem of sorrows, and we become better prepared to get to the root of the problem.

Chapter 11

Verse 11.1

Ashtavakra said,

"Transition of *being* and *non-being* takes place on its own,

convinced like this,

Devoid of afflictions; subsides blissfully."

In this verse, the word *being* refers to the state of material world post-creation, and the word *non-being* refers to the state of material world post-dissolution.

The transitions of creation and dissolution take place on their own. The person – who is convinced like this – becomes devoid of tribulations, and manages to subside his mind peacefully.

Doubt: But the creation seems to be an eternal phenomenon. How can we say that it gets created or dissolved?

Answer: By the evidence of scriptures. All ancient scriptures give a detailed account of the process of creation and dissolution.

For the enlightened person, however, the process of creation or dissolution does not remain a topic of interest, because he knows that such a process is as illusory as the *seen phenomenon.*

He becomes devoid of afflictions on account of his realization of the *real self.*

The real self is the formless existence which is peaceful by its very nature.

Verse 11.2

"God is the creator of all, no one else here, convinced like this,

Having dropped all expectations from within, peaceful, does not get attached anywhere."

The enlightened person understands it too well that an individual subject cannot be the doer – and certainly not the creator – of any manifestation.

All the individuals get driven by their destined karma, and they do not have any free will. In his understanding, therefore, he realizes that he is going to get his share of worldly pleasures and pains. This knowledge makes him peaceful internally.

Externally, he may seemingly take part in many activities, but internally, his mind subsides in peace due to this realization.

He, therefore, does not remain attached to the worldly activities, even while taking part in them.

Verse 11.3

"Times of prosperity and calamity come due to destiny, convinced like this,
Satisfied, with his senses, peaceful, neither does he expect nor grieves."

Since the enlightened person realizes himself as the witnessing consciousness, he takes things philosophically. Therefore, he does not get perturbed during the times of either prosperity or calamity, and quietly works out his destined karma day by day.

Verse 11.4

"Happiness and sorrow, birth and death happen due to destiny, convinced like this,
Devoid of *goal and effort*, while doing also, does not get stuck."

Happiness and sorrows are psychological conditions.

Birth and death are physical conditions.

The lifeform, the lifespan and the experiences are determined by the package of destined karma.

Therefore, the psychological and physical conditions occur due to the force of destined karma.

Realizing this, the enlightened person does not keep any personal agenda in the world. He, therefore, does not remain glued to objects.

Verse 11.5

"Sorrow comes through worry and not otherwise; convinced like this,
Free of that, becomes happy, peaceful, devoid of craving everywhere."

Worry is the result of apprehension. Apprehension is there when the sense of doer-ship is there.

The thinking that I am an individual self, and I am the subject of activities as their doer is the primary cause of all sorrows.

An enlightened person remains free of such a thinking. Therefore, he remains happy, peaceful and does not crave for anything.

Verse 11.6

"*I am not the body nor the body is mine, I am pure consciousness*, convinced like this,
Attains singularity, does not remember *non-deeds* and *deeds*."

Doubt: Does it mean that after realization, the enlightened person forgets his past?

Answer: Till the gross body of an enlightened person is alive, the intellect and the memory functions work normally.

The enlightened person does remember some of his past deeds from time to time.

He, however, does not tend to carry either regret or a sense of pride any longer vis-a-vis his past deeds.

He realizes that all the activities were caused by destined karma, and that he was never the doer of them because he was never the subject of karma; but, was always the pure consciousness.

Verse 11.7

"*From the creator to a blade of grass, everything is me only*, convinced like this,
Devoid of distractions, pure, peaceful, not concerned if he gets something or does not get it."

The all-pervasive formless existence is the *real self* of all animate and inanimate objects of the creation - from the *creator deity* to a blade of grass.

Having realized himself to be the formless existence, the wise does not get deluded or distracted by the activities around him. He always remains peaceful internally.

Since he remains devoid of cravings, he does not remain concerned if he gets something or doesn't get it.

Verse 11.8

"*Full of surprises, yet this universe is nothing really*, convinced like this,
Becomes devoid of desire, pure consciousness alone; subsides as though nothing."

The enlightened person realizes that the world is an appearance only and not a reality in itself.

Therefore, he becomes devoid of desires, realizes himself as the pure consciousness, and due to the absence of a personal agenda, his mind subsides in peace.

The word *nothing* should not be taken as *non-existence*, but it merely implies the *lack of subjectivity* on part of an enlightened person.

Chapter 12

Verse 12.1

Janaka said,

"First, aloof from the actions performed by the body, then aloof from the expanse of speech,

Now aloof from worry, I stay, just as I am."

With the increased understanding, Janaka has realized that actions performed by the body, and those by speech, are caused by destined karma.

He has also realized that his *real self* was never the subject of that karma.

He no longer has a reason to worry about the future because he has realized that at every given moment, it is the destined karma which is working itself out through the body, mind and speech; and that he need never be the subject of it.

Therefore, he stays just as he is: the peaceful and blissful pure consciousness.

Verse 12.2

"Due to lack of interest in words, knowing invisibility of the *self* too,

In spite of distractions in the heart, I stay just as I am."

Since Janaka has realized the pure consciousness as his *real self*, he does not find meaning and purpose in the worldly affairs any more. Therefore, he is no longer interested in the business of words which is merely an expanse of the speech function.

He realizes that the developments of the world do not entirely depend upon the spoken words, but they are more likely to happen as per the pre-programmed course of the destined karma.

He also realizes that the *real self* can only be understood by recognizing one's unity with it, and it can never be understood as an object of perception.

Even though due to the force of destined karma, his body and intellect are still active, but he realizes himself to be the witnessing consciousness which never becomes the subject of activities.

Therefore, he does not get perturbed by the distractions caused by the destined karma, and is able to remain peaceful internally.

Verse 12.3

"*Meditation and distraction*, this business is there for Samadhi,
Having looked at this rule, I stay just as I am."

Meditation is a practice which helps us achieve a stillness of mind for some time.

Distractions in the mind are caused by the force of destined karma.

Therefore, meditation and distractions keep on replacing each other. The practice of meditation is necessary to accomplish the state of Samadhi, which is the complete stillness of the mind, in which it remains in a state of one-pointed awareness.

However, the stillness achieved by such a practice always remains temporary, and vulnerable to distractions.

Hence, Janaka is not getting carried away by the practices such as meditation. Instead, he is so satisfied with the realization that has come through the words of Ashtavakra that he is able to stay as *pure consciousness* alone.

Doubt: Can the realization that comes through the words be temporary as well?

Answer: Realization means lack of doubts. Once the doubts vanish, then nothing can create further ignorance.

The doubts vanish when we realize the nature of our real self by evidenced-based knowledge. For example, when we mistakenly perceive a rope as a snake, that misperception can be dispelled by the words of our well-wisher that *the object is a rope and not a snake.*

The words of our well-wisher can act as evidence in this regard, which can help us understand the reality of that object.

The meditation and Samadhi can lead to self-realization according to *Yoga* philosophy, but then it has a different metaphysical framework altogether.

In the framework of non-dualism though, the primary means to self-realization remain the *understanding* that comes through the wisdom revealed by the realized sages in the verbal form. These words are present in the form of scriptures.

Verse 12.4

"Due to the lack of *acquisition and abandonment*, likewise *joy and grief*,
O *Brahman*, I just stay as I am."

Having understood the illusory nature of the *seen objects*, Janaka does not see much of a meaning and purpose with them.

Therefore, for him, nothing remains to be acquired; nor does anything remain to be abandoned.

Neither joy nor any disappointment.

Hence, he is able to stay just as he is - *pure consciousness.*

Verse 12.5

"The consideration of *a phase of life* or lack of such a consideration; the idea of *meditation or* the lack of it; the *mental acceptance or the mental rejection*;

Only distraction is seen by me in these; hence, I stay just as I am."

The phases of life can be childhood, student-hood, married life or monk-hood.

These phases - and the corresponding duties - matter to the person who sees himself as a worldly individual with subjectivity towards worldly affairs and experiences.

Similarly, for him, the ideas of acceptance and rejection of objects, based on inclinations of the mind, also remain relevant.

Janaka has realized himself as the *pure consciousness* which never has any subjectivity for the phenomenal world; therefore, the above-mentioned considerations and ideas do not matter to him any longer.

Verse 12.6

"Ritual is done due to ignorance, likewise it's abandonment,

Knowing this comprehensively, I stay just as I am."

The purpose of rituals is to generate merits for oneself, either to fulfill desires in this earthly life or to secure a place in heaven for the afterlife.

Since Janaka has got the nectar of immortality through the realization of the *real self*, he is no longer interested in traveling to a different world like heaven, by continuing to take himself as a worldly individual.

Hence, he does not see purpose in doing rituals.

However, he has also understood that all the actions, including rituals, take place due to the force of destined karma, therefore, he is not averse to doing them either. In any case, he would not have any real sense of purpose behind them.

Verse 12.7

"The *unthinkable*, when thought of, gets worshiped as *thinkable*,
Renouncing its contemplation, I stay just as I am."

This is a supreme state of understanding.

The ultimate reality, which is the formless and un-qualitative existence, can neither become an object of perception nor can it become an object of thinking. Therefore, it cannot be objectively contemplated upon either.

It can only be realized as our real self.

This realization is not a perceptual understanding, but a subjective realization: I am that.

When the doubts vanish, the mind ceases. Then, there remains nothing to be thought of, nor anything to be contemplated upon.

Total cessation of the mind due to the realization of the real self.

Verse 12.8

"Who has done it like this, he becomes fulfilled;
Whose essence is like this, he remains fulfilled."

The first line of this verse refers to those seekers who make an effort to realize the real self.

The second line refers to those seekers who have dropped the effort due to the correct understanding of the real self.

An ignorant person's understanding rides the outward tendency of his mind; and he tries to look for the truth outside of himself.

He does not realize that the outward ride of his mind is the biggest obstacle for *self-realization*; but if and when he realizes it, he makes a certain effort in the form of austerities and practices, to change the direction of the tendency, and makes it go inward.

Eventually, with the correct knowledge, he realizes that his *real self* is the formless existence, and all his efforts were only meant to drop the mind; and not to objectively get hold of the reality.

For the seekers like Janaka though, who have pure mind and sharp intellect, an effort is not required at all.

They can comprehend the truth merely through the words of wisdom; and can realize the formless existence as their *real self*, as soon as they are told so, verbally.

Chapter 13

Verse 13.1

Janaka said,

"*The world is nothing*, this kind of solace is rare even in monk-hood,

Renouncing abandonment and acquisition, I stay blissfully."

A monk remains bound by the customs of his order, and he also becomes a part of a certain hierarchy by virtue of his entry into the order. He is expected to maintain a certain lifestyle, including observance of the *Do's* and *Don'ts*, in order to maintain the holiness of that order. Due to it, his mind can remain occupied by a certain worldly perspective, and he may not get the leisure to solely focus on the wisdom of existential truth.

An enlightened person, on the other hand, knows it too well that the world is an illusory appearance and not a reality in itself.

He enjoys the solace and the leisure which is not there even in the monk-hood because he does not feel compelled to get driven by the ideas of *Do's* and *Don'ts.*

Therefore, he does not remain bound by the concepts of abandonment and acquisition either.

Verse 13.2

"Somewhere is a physical pain, tongue pains somewhere,

Somewhere does the mind; by giving up all these, I stay blissfully."

All the activities of the body, mind and speech involve some pain; and if pride gets attached with these activities, then they cause psychological pain too.

Knowing this, the enlightened person takes off his attention from the affairs of body, mind and speech; and just dwells in his realization of the *real self*.

Verse 13.3

"*Deeds* are nothing, knowing this principally,
When something needs to be done, doing that, I stay blissfully."

The body, mind and intellect of an individual person belong to the world of materials. Therefore, they are as illusory as the phenomenal world which creates them.

Knowing this, the enlightened person does not get attached to them, and he simply does what the force of destined karma makes him do, without getting subjectively attached to it.

That way, he stays in the bliss of his *real self* all the time.

Verse 13.4

"The concepts such as *action, inaction and restriction* are relevant for the *Yogis* staying in the body,
Due to detachment from conjunction and disjunction, I stay blissfully."

Those yogis who consider themselves as individual subjects, try to tranquil the mind through the practice of meditation. For that, they tend to give utmost importance to the observance of a certain lifestyle which includes concepts such as *action, inaction and restriction.*

An enlightened person, however, realizes himself to be the formless existence, therefore, he does not see any purpose in either actions, inactions or restrictions. He always stays in the bliss of his *real self* by virtue of his realization.

Verse 13.5

"Gain or loss, not mine, either by sitting, moving or sleeping;
Therefore, while sitting, moving or sleeping, I stay blissfully."

Since an enlightened person does not see any meaning and purpose in this illusory creation, he sees nothing to gain, nothing to prove or nothing to lose, either by means of an activity or by inactivity.

He simply allows his body to function as per the course of destined karma, without any subjective interference in it.

Verse 13.6

"Neither is any loss of mine by sleeping nor any gain by an effort,
Putting aside destruction and celebration, I stay blissfully."

Since an enlightened person does not consider himself to be an individual subject, he does not take himself as a duty-bound person. He carries on with his routine duties and jobs due to the force of destined karma, although internally he has nothing to gain from it.

He might show emotions or excitement at times, but internally he remains unaffected by it.

Therefore, in a way, he stays away from celebrations and grief.

Verse 13.7

"Having observed many times, no rule between objects and pleasures,
Putting aside the *auspicious and inauspicious*, I stay blissfully."

A person with a ritualistic approach tends to be obsessed with concepts such as *auspicious* and *inauspicious*.

Due to the obsession, he always tries to observe a certain degree of piousness and purity, in and around his behavior; hoping that such an observance will bring only nice experiences to him.

But it has been seen that the package of destined karma contains both types of experiences: *good* and *bad*.

It gives us both: moments of joy and moments of disappointment.

Even the people who maintain strict rules of piousness and purity have to face auspicious and inauspicious circumstances.

Similarly, it has also been seen that the same objects become the cause of happiness sometimes, and then the same objects become the cause of sorrow at other times.

Therefore, from a philosophical point of view, there is no direct rule of correlation as such between the objects and the pleasures.

Knowing this well, an enlightened person does not get overly obsessed with the ideas of *auspicious* and *inauspicious*; instead, he dwells in the bliss of his *real self*, by virtue of his realization of it.

Chapter 14

Verse 14.1

Janaka said,

"The one with essentially empty mind, dwells in the world mistakenly,
As if just awakened from the sleep, is surely free of the world."

The *'I'* of an enlightened person gets detached from psychology. Therefore, he essentially remains empty minded. He does not see any real purpose in the world, but till the destined karma gets fully worked out, his personality remains in the world as a normal individual personality. He deals with the world without any personal interest, as if like a person who has just awakened from sleep.

Verse 14.2

"Where is the money? Where are friends? Where are the enemies in the form of pleasure? for me;
Where is the scripture? Where is the knowledge too? When my craving has fallen off!"

The craving for pleasure binds us to the world. It makes us see meaning and purpose in this illusory world.

Craving for money, craving for friends, craving for pleasures and even craving for knowledge makes us see purpose and meaning in this dream creation; but now, with an increased understanding, Janaka recognizes it, and is able to drop the craving.

Doubt: It is all right to say that the craving for pleasures is bad, and it has been termed as *enemies* in the verse; but why is the craving for knowledge also a problem?

Answer: Initially, the craving for knowledge is better than the craving for pleasures, because knowledge liberates us from sorrows; but once we have a fair understanding of our *real self*, with a certain degree of conviction, then the knowledge is as useless as any other element. Knowledge is a thorn which serves as an aid to take out the thorn of ignorance. After that, both the thorns need to be dropped.

Janaka's understanding has reached to a level whereby he has dropped the purpose and meaning in this dream creation. Hence, he does not need to make a distinction between the *craving for pleasures* and the *craving for knowledge*.

Verse 14.3

"Knowing that *the witnessing principle in the self and in the God is the same*,
No worries for me in bondage or liberation, or for my salvation."

Janaka has amply realized that he was always the witnessing consciousness and was never a part of this dream creation; therefore, all the concepts such as *individuality, God, bondage and salvation* have become irrelevant for him.

Having attained this level of understanding, and the contentment thereby, he does not have any worries remaining, including that of liberation.

Doubt: If Janaka was always the witnessing consciousness, then why did he take himself as an individual subject for so long?

Answer: Technically speaking, the *why* is an illogical question because any answer to the previous *why* can again be asked with one more *why*.

The answer can be given analogically: Why does a dream come? It comes on its own as a mysterious effect. More so, the dream world matters to the one who takes himself either as the subject of it or as the participant in it; but after awakening, that subject or that participant simply vanishes along with the phenomenon itself.

Verse 14.4

"Internally free of distractions, externally fanciful like deluded;
Conditions of his are understood by only his kind of persons."

The enlightened person remains in the world only as long as his remaining destined karma of the current life gets worked fully.

Post-enlightenment, he can be seen as an impulsive person at times, sometimes eccentric, fanciful or sometimes mature.

His behavior, however, which can sometimes defy customary logic and norms, can be understood only by another self-realized person, who belongs to the same category.

Chapter 15

Verse 15.1

Ashtavakra said,

"By a little sermon gets satisfied, the one with a pure mind,
Lifelong curious, devoid of that, remains infatuated."

A person with a pure mind tends to realize the unity of his *real self* with the formless existence, even when told only a few words of wisdom.

On the other hand, a person who does not have a pure mind, requires the same truth to be stated in many ways and in many words; and even after that, he may take some more time to steep in the knowledge, and eventually realize the truth.

The knowledge is the same in both cases, but the purity level varies in different individuals, hence, the same knowledge may take a different length of time to make an individual realize the true nature of the *real self*.

Doubt: How does the mind become purer?

Answer: Thoughts are the most powerful means to purify the mind. If someone finds it difficult to draw a correct understanding from the thoughts, and if his mind sways too much, then he may try meditation or a little bit of austerities to calm down the mind, to be able to comprehend the understanding that arises with the thoughts.

Doubt: Does it mean that the knowledge works in tandem with the practices such as meditation and austerities?

Answer: No. Knowledge does not require alliance of any other practice, but the individual mind upon which the knowledge is supposed to work may require a little bit of austerities or meditation to remove the impurities which otherwise act as an obstacle for its comprehension.

Verse 15.2

"Lack of interest in pleasures is *liberation*, persistent interest in pleasures is *bondage*,
This much is the knowledge; do as you wish."

The persistent interest in pleasures keeps an ignorant individual attached to the phenomenal world. This attachment ensures the continuum of ignorance in that individual, and it keeps his *bondage* intact.

When that interest goes down, that individual gets into a better position to investigate into the nature of his *real self*. This *self-inquiry* weakens the bondage by reducing the sense of subjectivity in that individual; and eventually he realizes himself to be the formless existence, and stops seeing purpose in the world. Due to this enlightenment, he attains liberation.

Verse 15.3

"This realization turns a *speaking, conscious and busy person* into a *mute, inert* and *lethargic* one,
Therefore, it has been abandoned by the people who seek pleasures."

The people who seek pleasures from the phenomenal world remain very talkative, alert and busy in their activities; because they expect those activities to fetch happiness for them.

When, by any chance of destiny, they come in touch with the *wisdom of non-dualism*, they fear the eventual *loss of purpose.*

If they are not ready to drop their concepts of *right and wrong, good and bad, status, honor, prosperity and wealthy life*, then they conveniently dump this wisdom, and prefer to remain engaged in their worldly activities; seeking worldly pleasures, and chasing happiness by remaining occupied with their own concepts of *status, honor, and prosperity.*

On the other hand, an enlightened person wears this *loss of purpose* as a badge of honor on his shoulders, because he does not depend on the activities for his happiness; instead, he remains ever blissful due to his realization of the non-dual nature of the *real self.*

Therefore, he may sometimes be seen as a *mute, inert* or *lethargic* person; but it does not matter to him in any case.

This verse, however, does not proclaim being *mute, inert* or *lethargic* to be the necessary signs of enlightenment; but it just narrates the *lack of dependency* of an enlightened person on the activities, for having happiness.

Verse 15.4

"Neither you are the body nor the body is yours; nor are you the doer or enjoyer;
You are *pure consciousness*, always the *witness*, absolute one;
Move freely."

Due to the deep spell of ignorance, a person genuinely thinks that his *self* is the gross body.

When his understanding evolves a bit, then he tends to think that *he is an individual soul, and the body is his possession.*

Both propositions, however, are equally wrong.

Our being is neither an individual body, nor is it an individual soul.

Our *being* is an all-pervasive existence which is formless and un-qualitative in its nature.

Doubt: But when we use the term *'I'*, at that time we naturally tend to point towards our individual body.

Answer: When an ignorant person uses the term *'I'*, he genuinely implies that *his being is the gross body*; but when an enlightened person uses the term *'I'*, then it is more of a formality on his part, which he uses to carry out his routine communication.

Doubt: But we also use the term *'my body'*, and we mean it that way.

Answer: That is due to the ignorance that prevails in our intellect about the nature of our *real self.*

If the material body would really be a possession of an individual soul, then there would exist multiple souls. Such a proposition would imply that *God must have fragmented himself into multiple souls when he created them.* It would also imply that *God is a divisible existence.*

In that case, God would not remain as an infinite existence.

Also, multiple souls working for different purposes will limit the power and scope of *God;* which is clearly an absurd proposition, and it is not logical to believe so.

There is no consensus either amongst those who believe in the *individuality of the soul* about the dimensions and qualities of an individual soul.

On the other hand, going by the experiential approach, we can say that every individual - irrespective of his form and other time-place factors - gets the same general experience of *deep sleep* due to the *lack of mental activity* during the *deep sleep.*

It means that the active mind in the waking and dreaming states brings the false sense of individuality in these two states.

Therefore, the *individuality of the self* cannot be an absolute idea; and it prevails in the intellect only due to *ignorance.*

Verse 15.5

"Affection and hatred are the qualities of mind, and the mind is never yours,
Your *self* is devoid of distractions, pure consciousness, bliss;
Move freely."

Just like the body is not ours, the mind also does not belong to us, nor do we belong to the mind. It is due to *ignorance* that the *'I'* gets attached to the psychology of an individual.

Doubt: So where does the *'I'* belong?

Answer: *'I'* is just a concept of the intellect.

It arises in the intellect due to *ignorance* about the *real self.*

With the knowledge of the real self, the *'I'* subsides.

There is no expression such as *'I'* in the all-pervasive existence. The all-pervasive existence is a formless *being* who, in his pristine nature, never becomes the subject of functions or expressions.

Everything which appears in this dream creation, including the *'I'*, feels real because of the background presence of the all-pervasive existence; and the all-pervasive existence is the *real self* of all.

Verse 15.6

"The *self* is in all beings, all beings in the *self*,
Knowing this, devoid of *ego*, devoid of attachment; be blissful."

The Self in all beings and all beings in the self – is possible because the *self* is a reality and the forms are illusory.

The ego – the concept of *'I'* in an individual – is a false entity. It prevails due to *ignorance*.

Once the doubts about the *real self* vanish from the intellect, then the concept of *Individual 'I'* also vanishes.

Then, the worries and sorrows brought in by *individual 'I'* also vanish.

Therefore, Ashtavakra is asking Janaka to remain ever blissful by giving up the *ego*, and the attachment that came with it.

Doubt: If the *'I'* is unreal, then how does the *'I am that'* statement work?

Answer: During the contemplation of *'I am that'*, the *'I'* part and the *'that'* part get dropped eventually, and only *'am'* remains.

This *'am'* exists on its own, and it does not need expressions such as *'I'* or *'that'*.

Verse 15.7

"Where this universe springs, like waves in an ocean,
You are that, have no doubt, O consciousness, be free of anguish."

The formless existence is the foundation on which this illusory appearance of the universe is being seen.

That formless existence is the *real self* of all. Therefore, there is no need to have anguish or antipathy towards any entity of the phenomenal world.

Anguish comes when we take ourselves as individual selves who are the subjects of the phenomenal world and who have desires in the material world.

Verse 15.8

"Have faith, O Son, have faith, and have no infatuation here,
Consciousness you are, beyond the physical nature."

The physical nature is made up of twenty-three metaphysical elements:
the intellect,
the ego (a material fabric that generates pride),
eleven sensory elements,
five sub-atomic elements,
five gross elements.

(Note: Only in the commentary of this verse, the word 'ego' implies a metaphysical material fabric; elsewhere in the book, it invariably implies 'the pride').

These metaphysical elements are inert materials because they do not have the ability to recognize the experiences on their own.

On the other hand, the *real self* is *pure consciousness*, which is a *non-material* reality, and which has the ability to recognize the experiences on its own. This ability is the default nature of the *real self*.

In non-dualism, the *real self* is the only real existence, and the rest of the metaphysical elements are illusory phenomena.

Infatuation in the physical objects prevails as long as *ignorance* prevails; but, when the doubts about the *real self* vanish, then the infatuation also gets dropped due to the recognition of illusory nature of material elements.

Verse 15.9

"Encircled by qualities, the body, stays, comes and goes,
The *real self*, neither goes nor comes, why do you grieve for it?"

Since the gross body is made up of metaphysical elements, it has its own course to complete as per the destined karma. Therefore, it comes, stays and perishes when its course is complete.

The *real self*, however, is an omnipresent reality. It never comes because it remains present as an eternal existence. It never goes because it is immortal, and it does not depend on anything else for its existence.

A person finds a reason to grieve only as long as he does not realize the true nature of the *real self*; but once he discovers it, then he becomes immortal himself, and does not grieve for material loss.

Verse 15.10

"May the body stay till the end of creation or may it perish right now,
Where is the gain or loss for the *pure consciousness you*?"

In this verse Ashtavakra is narrating the fact that the *real self* is *pure consciousness*; and that is our real *being*.

It does not perish even when the body perishes, because it is an eternal existence.

Therefore, the death of our physical body does not mean the end of our existence.

We shall continue to exist as an eternal *pure consciousness*, with or without the gross body.

Verse 15.11

"In the infinite ocean of your *being*, this wave of the universe,
May rise or set on its own; neither gain nor loss for you."

The entire universe is a creation of twenty-three metaphysical elements. It appears as a phenomenon like a dream appears, stays, and gets dissolved into a fundamental metaphysical element on its own.

If we realize our *real self* to be the omnipresent *pure consciousness*, then, for us, there remains nothing to be gained or lost by virtue of manifestation or dissolution of the material universe.

Verse 15.12

"O Son, you are *pure consciousness* only, the world is not different from you,
Therefore, for Whom? How? Where? - are the concepts such as *abandonment* or *acquisition*?"

The world is not different from the *real self* in the sense that the *real self* is the existential foundation in which this phenomenal world appears, like a dream phenomenon appears in the mind of a dreamer.

Therefore, we being that *real self*, have no reason to remain obsessed with the concepts such as *abandonment* or *acquisition*.

Verse 15.13

"In the one, indivisible, peaceful, *pure consciousness* you,
Where is birth, karma, and where is ego also?"

In the *real self* which is the all-pervasive formless existence, there is no scope for birth or karma to take place in reality, because the formless existence is the only real existence.

The creation and its activities including the birth and karma, are illusory appearances.

Since an enlightened person realizes himself to be *pure consciousness* alone, therefore he tends to become devoid of ego.

Verse 15.14

"Whatever you see, there, you only get perceived,
Can the ring and the bracelet be perceived separately from the gold?"

We cannot perceive the ring or the bracelet independent of its material cause – the gold.

When we perceive the ring or the bracelet, we perceive the gold only, but in a certain form.

If we take out the names and forms out of the ring and the bracelet, still the gold remains there as the material element; because the cause can exist independent of its effect, but an effect cannot exist independent of its material cause.

The forms of the phenomenal world are the effects, and the formless existence the cause; and since the formless existence is our *real self*, therefore, when we perceive the forms of the world, at that time essentially, we perceive their cause, which is the *real self*.

Doubt: The ring or the bracelet are the transformations of gold. Does it mean that the forms of the world are also transformations of the formless existence?

Answer: No. In non-dualism, an *effect* is *not* considered as a transformation of the cause; but it is considered as a *distorted perception* of the cause; because the forms – as the effects – are illusory appearances, and the formless existence – as the cause – is the only reality.

Verse 15.15

"Abandon the division such as '*this is me and this is not me*', *Everything is self*, having got convinced like this, devoid of vow, be blissful."

Doubt: If everything is *self*, then why don't we perceive everything as '*I*'?

Answer: The '*I*' is a concept that gets generated by ignorant intellect due to its *ignorance* about the real nature of the *self*.

'I' is not an expression that originates from the formless existence in actuality. In fact, there is no real expression that originates from the formless existence.

Doubt: Then why to believe in the presence of that existence?

Answer: Because we perceive everything in terms of *'is-ness'*.

We perceive our individual persona and other objects in terms of *'am', 'is' and 'are'*.

We don't perceive them in terms of *'not am'* and *'not are'*.

More so, the *'is-ness'* can never be taken away from the objects even when they change their appearance.

It means that beneath the names and forms of the objects, there exists a *reality* that remains ever present irrespective of the changes that occur in the names and forms.

That *reality* is the formless existence, which is omnipresent, eternal and indivisible existence; and it never becomes the subject of the phenomenal world made up of names and forms.

Since that formless existence is our *real self*, therefore, the distinction of *'I', 'you' and 'it'* remains relevant only in the domain of names and forms; but it becomes redundant in the realm of existence.

Verse 15.16

"Due to your *ignorance*, the world is there; spiritually, only *you are*,
There is nothing apart from *you*, either worldly or transcendentally."

Due to the 'I' concept that arises in the intellect of an individual, the distinction between 'I' and 'this' becomes relevant for him; but when the doubts about the real self vanish, the distinction between 'I' and *'this'* also vanishes. Then there remains only one attribute-less existence.

Verse 15.17

"*Illusion only is this universe, substantially nothing*; like this the convinced one,
Becomes devoid of passions, and subsides as if *nothing*."

In this verse, the word *nothing* implies the *cessation of mind*. It should not be taken as a negation of an ultimate reality, because existence *cannot* be *nothing*.

Existence is a term that indicates a certain *presence*.

Verse 15.18

"Only one was, is and will be, in the ocean of this world;
Neither your bondage is there nor liberation. Having done with it, move on blissfully."

The formless existence remains present before, during and after the occurrence of the illusory appearance of the phenomenal world.

The bondage, in the form of the *'I'* concept, is also a part of that illusion. Therefore, the bondage never existed as a reality.

The *ignorance* about the *real self* is the *bondage*, and the correct understanding about it, is *liberation*.

The *ignorance* and the *understanding*, both are non-material entities. They exist as effects, without being there in substance.

Therefore, as a metaphysical reality, only the *real self* exists; in the past, present and future also.

Verse 15.19

"Do not excite your mind with vows and distractions, *O Consciousness*,
By subsiding them, stay happy in the blissful idol of the *self*."

The *self* is an idol of bliss because it is an eternal source of the *joy of being existent*; and that is our real nature.

This *joy of being existent* is the basic lifeline for everyone and everything.

This reality, however, can be understood only by removing the obstacle from our intellect that prevents us from realizing this; and that obstacle is *ignorance*.

As long as *ignorance* prevails, we continue to take ourselves as the individual subjects of phenomenal experiences, and that gives rise to the creation of vows and distractions in our minds.

Therefore, Ashtavakra wants Janaka to remain in the bliss of his *real self*, and not attach himself to the vows and distractions of the mind.

Verse 15.20

"Abandon attention from everywhere, do not hold anything in the heart,
The *self* you are, eternally free by virtue of your nature; what will you do by thinking too much?"

Self-realization is not a result that gets newly produced by some thinking process.

Self-realization dawns when we pay attention to the fact that the *real self* – as the formless existence – is a pre, mid and post condition that remains ever present as an existential foundation of the thinking process.

Chapter 16

Verse 16.1

Ashtavakra said,

"Read or listen, Son, many scriptures many times,
But there will not be peace for you without *forgetting* everything."

In this verse, the word forgetting implies paying attention within and not outside.

Knowledge gained from the scriptures has to be understood inside us and not outside.

We can only realize the *real self* within ourselves, in terms of '*I am that*'; and not outside of ourselves.

Ashtavakra is making us aware that the object that the scriptures point to is really the existential foundation of the subject; and that foundation exists prior to the occurrence of mental processes.

That existential foundation is our real self. This real self is peaceful by the very nature of it.

Verse 16.2

"Indulgence, action or meditation, you may do, O knowledgeable,
But you will be truly delighted when all the expectations will vanish from your mind."

We indulge in pleasures through action, and get exhausted eventually. After that, we feel the need for meditation to calm the mind.

True delight, however, comes not when the mind is engaged either in activity or in meditation, but when it becomes devoid of all expectations.

The mind can become devoid of all expectations only by means of proper understanding of the *real self*.

Verse 16.3

"Due to the efforts, all are sorrowful; nobody knows this;
By this much sermon only, a renunciate achieves fulfillment."

Under the spell of ignorance, one gets engaged in activity, in order to obtain happiness.

The activity requires effort, and the effort makes a subject pay attention to the object he is dealing with; but even after that, the subject cannot obtain eternal happiness; because the result produced by means of an activity always remains temporary.

On the other hand, a renunciate can pull his mind back from the objects easily, and he can engage it in *self-inquiry*.

Therefore, a little sermon about the futility of effort becomes good enough for him to bring his attention back towards his *real self*, and subsequently he achieves fulfillment due to *self-realization*.

Verse 16.4

"He, who regrets even a small activity like blinking of an eyelid,
To that champion of laziness comes the happiness, not to anyone else."

A person who loses purpose in transactional activity by virtue of his understanding of the *real self*, does not remain motivated to get involved in the activity, internally or externally.

For him, sometimes, to carry out his routine activity may also become tedious. Therefore, Ashtavakra calls him *a champion of laziness*.

This verse, however, does not advocate laziness as a mandatory policy for realization; but it only points at the total loss of purpose of an enlightened person in the transactional world due to his realization of its illusory nature.

It is perfectly possible for him to remain very active in the world due to the force of his remaining destined karma.

However, in any case, he will not see any real purpose in the activity, and will allow the destined karma to work itself out through his personality; but, without taking himself as the subject of the karma or its results.

Verse 16.5

"*This is done and this is not done*, when the mind becomes free of the duo,
Then it becomes *non-expectant* vis-a-vis ritual, money, desire, liberation."

The duo of *done* and *not done* is there till the mind sees purpose in the world.

When – with the understanding of real self – the purpose gets dropped, then the duo of *done* and *not done* subsides. After that, the mind does not hanker after rituals, money, desire and liberation too.

Verse 16.6

"A dispassionate person hates pleasure, a passionate one craves for them,
But a person devoid of concepts such as *acquisition* or *renunciation*, neither remains dispassionate nor passionate."

A dispassionate mind hates the pleasures because it thinks that passions are the source of bondage.

A passionate mind seeks pleasures because it thinks that pleasures are the source of happiness.

Both of them, however, miss the point about the source of bondage and that of happiness:

The source of bondage is *ignorance*, which is essentially a lack of clarity about the nature of the real *self*.

The source of happiness is the *joy of being* that emanates from the formless existence.

An enlightened person understands it; therefore, he does not remain obsessed with the pleasures, nor does he hate them.

Verse 16.7

"*Abandonment* and *acquisition* are there till the tree of the world blossoms,
Craving remains alive till the *condition of thoughtlessness* comes."

As long as an ignorant mind sees purpose in the world, it gives importance to the concepts of *abandonment* and *acquisition*.

Till then, the mind seeks either renunciation or indulgences.

This craving of the mind remains till the futility of it is understood by the intellect.

Thereafter, and due to *self-realization*, the purpose gets dropped; and a *condition of thoughtlessness* arrives.

This *condition of thoughtlessness* does not occur as a result of a practice, but it occurs as a consequence of *self-realization.*

More so, one should not confuse this *thoughtlessness* with *dumbness.* This *thoughtlessness* indicates the *loss of subjectivity* on part of an enlightened person vis-a-vis the worldly experiences and perspectives.

Verse 16.8

"Attachment takes birth in activity, Aversion takes birth in inactivity,
Devoid of the duo, like a child, the wise one stays indifferent."

An activity requires a certain worldly material for the accomplishment of its objective.

In order to get that material and to fulfill the requirements of the objective, the mind craves for the resources that it believes are going to help it achieve the objective.

Therefore, all the activities bring attachment to the mind.

On the other hand, a person who hates activity, tries to remain away from it thinking that the activity involves the danger of binding him to the world. Therefore, he opts for the opposite end, and starts hating the activity.

The enlightened person, due to his correct understanding about the source of bondage, simply does not bother about the duel of *activity and inactivity.*

His attention remains towards the *real self*, and it helps him stay neutral to the effects of activity.

Therefore, he takes up an activity when it is warranted by the force of his destined karma, like a child does its activity without any preconditioning.

Verse 16.9

"A person with attachments, wants to abandon the world to get rid of the sorrow;
The unattached one remains free of sorrows, does not regret in that as well."

A person wants to abandon the world because he thinks that the world is the cause of his attachment. He does not realize that the attachment stays in his mind and not in the outside world.

On the other hand, an enlightened person simply understands the nature of his *real self*, and no longer remains attached to the mind.

Therefore, he remains free of sorrows by the very nature of his, and does not regret even while being in the world; and he just works out his remaining destined karma as and how it comes.

Verse 16.10

"A person who takes pride in the salvation and has an affection for the body as well,
Is neither a yogi, nor an enlightened being, and only becomes sorrowful."

Sometimes the knowledge of scholarly people remains restricted to the intellectual level, and it does not get converted into *self-realization* because of the importance they attach to their personalities due to their desire for social recognition.

Therefore, it generates pride in them.

Subsequently, they become sorrowful.

Verse 16.11

"Your preacher may be *Lord Shiva, or Lord Vishnu* or the lotus-born *Brahma*,
Yet, you will not have peace without forgetting all."

In this verse, the word *forgetting* implies *to look inwards and not to look outwards.* The real peace is attained when we realize the formless existence to be our *real self* within ourselves.

Therefore, it is not so much about the greatness of our teacher, but it is more about our own *self-discovery*, that happens subjectively by an inquiry of the existential foundation of our *being*.

Chapter 17

Verse 17.1

Ashtavakra said,

"By him the fruit of knowledge and the fruit of yoga has been received,

Who remains satisfied, pure in his senses, and always dwells alone."

The fruit of knowledge is *freedom*; and the fruit of yoga is *quietude of mind.*

An enlightened person attains *freedom* and *quietude* too.

He does not get driven by the sensory pleasures; hence, he remains pure in his senses.

Doubt: How come knowledge gives the fruit of yoga also? Yoga requires practice of meditation.

Answer: The *knowledge about the real self* is unique in its nature, and it is different from the *knowledge of worldly objects.*

The *knowledge about the real self* pulls the mind back towards the *real self*, and the real self remains in eternal quietude by virtue of its very nature; because it never becomes the subject of phenomenal experiences, and exists as a singularity.

The phrase '*always dwells alone*' in this verse refers to '*it's being the existential singularity*'.

Verse 17.2

"Oh, never in this world a wise person regret,

Only by him alone, is the universe pervaded."

The formless existence is all-pervasive.

An enlightened person realizes the formless existence to be his *real self*.

More so, he also recognizes that the actions of the body are caused by the destined karma.

He does not see a reason to endure regret because he realizes that his *real self* does not have any subjectivity vis-a-vis the karma.

Verse 17.3

"No indulgences bring joy to the self-relaxing wise one,
Just like the neem leaves to an elephant who is fond of sweet leaves."

The worldly indulgences are like neem leaves, which look fresh green and smell energetic, but are very bitter in taste.

On the other hand, the joy that comes from the knowledge of the *real self* is like the taste of sweet leaves.

The elephant who has tasted both - the neem leaves and the sweet leaves - understands the deceptive nature of the fresh green neem leaves.

Being aware of the end result - the bitter taste, he does not get attracted towards the neem leaves, and only prefers the sweet leaves.

Similarly, the wise one, having understood the joy that comes from the realization of the real self, always relaxes in his understanding of the real self, and does not get attracted towards the worldly indulgences which are as deceptive in nature as the neem leaves.

Verse 17.4

"A person who does not linger over the experience of indulgences after they are over,
and remains *non-aspirational* in the indulgences that he has not got; rare is a person like him."

An enlightened person may sometimes step in into the sphere of worldly indulgences due to the force of his remaining destined karma; however, he does not linger over the pleasures that those indulgences might have brought to him.

Pleasures may come to him as per his destined karma but he does not chase them as a pleasure seeking subject. Neither does he linger over the experience of the past pleasures nor does he romanticize the future pleasures. He simply allows his destined karma to work itself out through the body with minimal psychological intervention.

That minimal psychological intervention also is caused by the force of his destined karma.

The enlightened person understands it completely in his intellect, and he does not attach himself to those indulgences as their *subject.*

Verse 17.5

"The *pleasure-seeker* as well as the *liberation-seeker*, both are seen in this world;
Not aspiring for the pleasure or the liberation; rare is such a great person."

The *outward-looking* tendency of mind remains equally effective in the *pleasure-seekers* as well as in the *liberation-seekers.*

This tendency becomes the biggest source of sorrow for the *pleasure-seekers*, and the same tendency becomes the biggest obstacle for the *liberation-seekers.*

An enlightened person understands the fact that the source of happiness - and the source of liberation - is not outside; but the happiness and liberation are the very nature of our *real self*; therefore, he loses the sense of meaning and purpose in the creation.

Only some rare person recognizes this secret, therefore Ashtavakra calls him a *rare great person.*

Verse 17.6

"Rituals, money, desire, liberation, life and death likewise,
Neither of these remain worthy of acquisition or renunciation,
for the generous wise person."

An enlightened person understands that the *formless existence* is his *real self*, hence, he does not see any purpose in performing rituals either *to get more money* or *to fulfill more desires* or *to seek liberation* or *to extend his lifespan.*

He becomes convinced in his intellect that everybody and everything gets driven by the destined karma, and therefore he remains content in this understanding.

Verse 17.7

"Neither keeps a desire to dissolve the world, nor keeps hatred for its present state,
Whichever way he is able to make his living, from that alone gets fully satisfied."

Having understood the unreality of the illusory appearance of the world and its objects, an enlightened person never has any problems with the world, its affairs and its objects.

He merely witnesses his destined karma being worked out through the body. Therefore, he neither hankers after desires to become rich nor does he fantasize going to the mountains to lead an ascetic life.

He remains content with whatever is offered to him by life and destiny.

Verse 17.8

"*By this knowledge I am gratified*; remains like this with the subsided mind,
While seeing, listening, touching, smelling and tasting; stays happy."

With the knowledge of the *real self*, the mind of an enlightened person subsides - not metaphysically, but as a subject.

Then comes a great solace. The quest concludes and peace prevails. That creates a sense of gratification in his mind for this knowledge.

After which, while performing actions also, the sense of fulfillment prevails, and that leads him to stay happy all the time.

Verse 17.9

"Zero-sum vision, worthless efforts and the dull senses,
Neither desire nor renunciation, once the ocean of the world subsides."

An enlightened person, who has realized himself to be the source of all happiness, dwells in his realization effortlessly.

He realizes himself to be the witness of the play of destiny.

Neither does he set any goals for himself, nor does he require any vision to accomplish them; nor does he get driven by sensory happiness.

For him, the illusory ocean of the world subsides forever.

Verse 17.10

"Neither wakes nor sleeps, nor opens eyelids nor closes them,
Oh! An enlightened person lives in a somewhat peculiar condition."

The waking and deep sleep are states of the mind. During a 24-hour cycle of day and night, the mind transits between these states as per the karmic requirement.

Opening and closing of eyelids are actions of the body caused by the circulation of air within the body.

The *'I'* of an ignorant person remains attached to the body, and to the mind. He carries a strong sense of doer-ship, and considers himself to be the doer of all actions.

An enlightened person, however, realizes himself as the formless existence, and his *'I'* does not remain attached to the individual subject with a body-mind complex.

He realizes that he is neither the doer of bodily activity, nor is he the doer of mental activity.

The actions of the body and those of the mind both are caused by the force of destined karma.

Therefore, Ashtavakra says that the state of an enlightened person cannot be described perfectly in words, and therefore he appears to be living in a peculiar condition.

Doubt: Does it mean that enlightenment is a peculiar mental state?

Answer: In the case of an enlightened person, the words *state* or *condition* refer to his *understanding of the real self*, and they do not indicate any mental or physical condition.

Verse 17.11

"Everywhere remains fine, everywhere pure hearted,
Free of desires, the liberated person shines everywhere."

An enlightened person remains fine everywhere in all situations due to the lack of *subjective intervention* from his side.

He remains pure hearted because he does not keep any malicious intentions.

Therefore, he *shines everywhere* with his understanding of the real self.

Verse 17.12

"While seeing, listening, touching, smelling, eating, holding, speaking and roaming,
Free of desires, *the great one* remains free always."

An enlightened person always remains free due to the lack of desires in his heart vis-a-vis this illusory world.

Therefore, Ashtavakra describes him as *the great one.*

Verse 17.13

"Neither criticizes nor praises, neither gets joyous nor gets angry,
Neither gives nor takes;
The liberated person remains disinterested everywhere."

An enlightened person never becomes a party to the actions performed by his body, mind and speech due to the lack of subjectivity on his part.

Therefore, in essence, he neither criticizes nor praises, neither gets joyous nor gets angry, nor gives nor takes.

Verse 17.14

"Seeing a passionate lady or when death is near,
Unexcited and stable, *the great one* always remains free."

In the case of a self-realized person, the psychological intervention remains minimal in the affairs of the body.

Since he does not crave for the sensory pleasures, he does not get excited with the appeal of a passionate lady.

Since he does not see any purpose in this illusory world, and realizes that death is bound to come when the destined karma gets over, he does not get scared even during the last hours of his life.

Verse 17.15

"In happiness, in sorrow, in men, in women, in wealth and in poverty also,
Nothing special for the enlightened person, who remains indifferent everywhere."

An enlightened person remains indifferent to everything and everywhere because he does not see meaning in this illusory appearance of the world.

Verse 17.16

"Neither violence nor compassion, neither arrogance nor timidity,

Neither surprise nor excitement, in a person for whom the world has subsided."

An enlightened person does not see meaning and purpose in this illusory world, therefore, the world and its affairs do not hold power to have any effect on him. In a way, the world subsides for him.

Verse 17.17

"Liberated person neither hates the sensory pleasure nor craves for it,
With an unattached mind, he enjoys both: *getting and not getting*."

An enlightened person remains in a permanent state of joy because he realizes himself as the source of all happiness.

He also realizes that he is bound to get his share of material objects and pleasures as per his destined karma.

Hence, he remains blissful in both: *getting and not getting*, without becoming anxious about it.

Verse 17.18

"Satisfaction, dissatisfaction, profit-loss concepts,
Subsided mind does not know, stays as if singular."

The formless existence is a singularity which is one without any second.

The *'I'* of an enlightened person gets dissolved into that existence – not metaphysically, but as the subject. Therefore, the sense of duality does not remain real for him.

Hence, his mind does not seek satisfaction through external means, nor does it need to abide by the concepts such as *profit and loss.*

Verse 17.19

"Devoid of attachments and ego; convinced that *the world is not a reality,*
All his hopes dissolve; Performs not, even while performing."

An enlightened person becomes devoid of ego because his *'I'* gets dissolved into *pure consciousness.*

His sense of meaning also goes down with the understanding that *the world is an illusory appearance.*

He also understands that all the actions of the body and mind are caused by the force of destined karma, and that *he is not the doer of those.*

Therefore, he performs not even while performing them.

Verse 17.20

"Devoid of the *light, infatuation, dream* and *inertia,*
He attains a peculiar state with a subsided mind."

In this verse, *light* implies *intellectual knowledge.*

Dream and *inertia* imply *ignorance.*

These kinds of pairs of opposites are relevant for the one who seeks something outside of himself ignoring the ever-blissful nature of his *real self.*

An enlightened person, with his understanding of the *real self,* does not seek anything outside of himself. In a way, he remains aloof from the duel of *knowledge and ignorance.*

Hence, Ashtavakra describes his state as a peculiar state.

The word state points to his understanding, and not to his physical or mental condition.

Chapter 18

Verse 18.1

Ashtavakra said,

"Till whose realization, remains the dream-like illusion,
Prostrations to that singularly blissful and peaceful light."

Having elaborated on the nature of the real self in a variety of ways, now Ashtavakra begins to expound the ultimate stage: the surrender of an enlightened person that occurs with the total loss of subjectivity, due to realization of the *self*.

Till we realize the formless existence as our *real self*, the illusion of this dream-like world continues to produce its effect on us.

The moment we understand that our *self* is the *eternal existence*, the illusion ceases for us; in the sense that it no longer remains capable of having its effect on us, and it cannot make us sorrowful any longer.

In this verse, the word *prostration* implies *the surrender that comes with self-realization.*

Verse 18.2

"Earning all the money and getting many indulgences,
Still without renouncing all, one will not be blissful."

In this verse, the word renouncing implies understanding the fallacy of worldly objects and that of the pleasures they bring.

The world can be renounced by the realization of its illusory nature. After that, the real bliss dawns.

Verse 18.3

"Burnt by the flames of duty and sorrows; for the inner soul,
From where the calming bliss will come without drinking the
stream of nectar."

The *stream of nectar* is the knowledge of the *real self.*

Under the spell of ignorance, one takes himself as an individual subject who has duties and purpose in the world.

This misconception about the *real self* leads him to become sorrowful and miserable in the world; but when he realizes that he was never an individual subject, and that he was always *pure consciousness*, then the *sense of being duty-bound* does not remain predominant in him.

Therefore, sorrows tend to disappear for him.

From the perspective of others, he will still be seen as a person who performs his routine actions normally, and that is due to the force of his remaining destined karma; but internally he will not remain bound by the sense of duty or purpose.

Doubt: Post *self-realization*, does the destined karma influence physical actions alone or does it influence the psychology too?

Answer: The destined karma tends to influence both: the physical actions and the psychology too. The difference, however, that comes due to *self-realization* is that the enlightened person understands that his *real being* is *pure consciousness*, whereas the ignorant person continues to confuse his *being* with an individual subject and its psychological character.

Therefore, the *being* of the ignorant person, in his own perspective, continues to be the subject of sorrows and miseries; while the *being* of the enlightened person does not remain so.

Verse 18.4

"This world is a perceived reality, and nothing in itself from the spiritual standpoint;
Never is there an absence of either the perceived reality or the spiritual reality."

The world is only a perceived reality because it exists as an appearance, and not as a substance.
The substance is the spiritual *self*, which is the pure conscious existence.
Since the world is not a reality in itself, it cannot physically vanish either; the phenomenon of dream remains as long as the person who is dreaming it continues to perceive it.

Verse 18.5

"Neither far away nor at a close distance, this *real self*,
Devoid of alternatives, effortless, unchanging and spotless."

The *real self* is not an object of space-time phenomenon. It is the subject of it, that too, under the spell of ignorance.
In actuality, the *real self* is a formless existence which is the foundation of space-time.
Therefore, the space related measurements are not applicable to it.
It cannot be said to be *far away* or *very near* spatially.
The foundation is only one hence it exists without any alternatives.
It is effortless because it is complete.
It is unchanging because it is non-transformative.
It is spotless because it remains untouched by impurities.
Doubt: Why can't the subject be different for every individual creature like in psychology? Why can't the *real self* of an individual person be separate from that of other people?

Answer: Because the *sense of being* is the same for everyone. The *is-ness* which is felt by everybody is the same. So, the source of it must also be the same.

As we have seen earlier, the duality is perceived only during the waking and dream state when the mind remains active.

In deep sleep, the mind does not remain active, therefore the sense of duality subsides temporarily; that brings an unqualified experience of relaxation; and this unqualified experience is felt the same by all individuals irrespective of their gender, age or lifeform.

Therefore, the *real self* who is the *pure conscious existence,* and also the source of *is-ness,* is only *One* and it is same for all individuals.

Verse 18.6

"With the dissolution of infatuation and with the knowledge of the *real self*,
The veil of ignorance ceases to exist and the wise shines devoid of grief."

The dissolution of infatuation and the knowledge of the *real self*, are two sides of the same coin.

With the understanding of the *real self*, the sense of reality in the world goes down. Hence, infatuation also reduces. This understanding about the *real self* dispels the veil of ignorance.

Verse 18.7

"Everything is an imagination only; the *real self* is *ancient* and *free*,
Having known this, what shall the brave one practice as if a child would do?"

In this verse, the word *ancient* implies *being permanent.*

Our mind creates the concept of time when it recognizes a change around it. The *real self*, which is a motionless reality, exists beyond time.

Therefore, in reality, it is neither ancient nor modern. It exists as a singularity, and remains present irrespective of the manifestation or dissolution of the time-space phenomenon.

Verse 18.8

"*Self is the all-pervasive existence and rest everything is imaginary*, convinced like this,
What more should the desire-less person know? talk? and do?"

The appearance of the world is based on the foundation of the formless existence. Having understood that existence as the *real self*, an enlightened person becomes desire-less.

He does not seek happiness outside of himself any longer, either by knowing more, talking more or doing more things.

Verse 18.9

I am this and *I am not this,* these concepts have dimmed,
Of the peaceful being, having got convinced that *All is self.*

The existential foundation of all forms is the pure conscious existence. Having understood that existence as the *self*, the sense of individuality of an enlightened person goes down.

Therefore, his idea of *self* no longer remains confined to a particular individual form, and sense of duality also vanishes from his intellect.

Verse 18.10

"Neither distraction nor concentration, neither knowledge nor foolishness,

Neither happiness nor sorrow, for the subsided being."

An enlightened being does not feel the need to rely on a particular mental trait to become happy. Therefore, he does not feel the need to rely on meditation techniques.

The distractions of the mind do not remain a problem for him any longer since he realizes himself as the witnessing consciousness of the psychological transitions such as concentration and distraction.

He does not feel the need to seek more information regarding the *real self*, hence the need for the knowledge also wanes away for him.

Verse 18.11

"In sovereignty or in beggar-hood, in profit or in loss, in public or in a forest,
Nothing special for an enlightened person who remains distraction-less by nature."

An enlightened person realizes the formless existence as his *real self*. Therefore, he does not get carried away by worldly notions such as authority, richness or poverty.

He remains indifferent whether he is dwelling in a city or in a jungle. He understands the non-transformative nature of the *real self*, therefore he remains essentially distraction-less.

Verse 18.12

"Where is the ritual, where is the desire, where is the money and where is the discrimination,
For the liberated person who remains free of duality such as this is done and this is not done."

The *duel* of *this is done* and *this is not done* stays in the mind of a person who sees purpose in the world due to his *sense of being an individual subject.*

An enlightened person does not see that; therefore, he remains free of the *duel.*

Verse 18.13

"No duty as such nor any passion in the heart,
Whichever way life goes on, the liberated person simply lives it that way."

Ignorance, coupled with desire, creates passion.

The liberated one, with the correct understanding of the *real self*, dispels the ignorance which makes him a desireless person.

The psychological intervention reduces. He simply lives by the force of remaining destined karma; as and how it takes him forward in the course of life.

Verse 18.14

"Where is the infatuation or where is the universe, where is the cognizance of the world and where is the freedom,
For the *great soul* who is resting beyond all *resolves.*"

An ignorant mind sees a purpose in the world, and the purpose gives rise to *a resolve*; but in the case of a *self-realized* person, the *stimulus* which gives rise to *a resolve* becomes ineffective.

The great liberated person essentially rests beyond all resolves due to his loss of purpose that comes from the knowledge of its illusory nature.

Verse 18.15

"The one who sees the universe, may he try to negate it,
But what will he do who sees it not even while seeing it?"

An ignorant person sees the world as a real phenomenon.

When he becomes a liberation-seeker, he may find it pertinent to negate its reality, for the sake of his enlightenment, and also to drive his point in scholarly discussions; but a *self-realized* person - who is convinced of its illusory nature, and who does not have sense of reality in it - does not even bother to negate the world, because he realizes that the world cannot affect his *being* which happens to be the formless existence.

This is the peak of spiritual understanding.

Verse 18.16

"A person who sees the all-pervasive existence as a *separate being* from his *self*, may he contemplate *I am that*,
But the one who does not see a second one, what should he contemplate?"

An ignorant person starts contemplating on the scriptural sentences such as *I am that*, believing that such a contemplation will lead to his *self-realization*; but as long as the sense of individuality in him remains strong, which brings the distinction of *I* and *That*, he remains far away from the truth.

On the other hand, the wise one drops his sense of individuality, and realizes the all-pervasive existence as his *real self*. After that he stops seeking everything - materially and spiritually.

Therefore, he does not feel the need to contemplate on scriptural sentences such as *I am that*.

The scriptural wisdom is relevant for the one who is under the spell of *ignorance*; but once *self-realization* dawns, even scriptures become redundant.

Verse 18.17

"A person who feels distracted from the *self*; may he meditate;

But a great one never gets distracted, what should he do in the absence of an aim?"

An ignorant mind needs meditation because it gets affected by the external and internal distractions; but a *self-realized* person, who has realized himself as the *witnessing consciousness* of the mind, never gets affected by the distractions of the mind.

Verse 18.18

"A *courageous person* remains different from worldly people, even while present amongst them,

He does not see meditation, distraction or karmic coating of himself."

As a metaphysical element, the mind either meditates or remains distracted; also, it gets colored by the karmic effects and their results.

A self-realized person does not get colored by the karma because he realizes himself to be the witness of the mind.

Therefore, for him, the concepts such as meditation, distraction and karmic coating do not matter.

Verse 18.19

"Free of concepts such as *presence* and *absence*, a dispassionate person,

Nothing gets done by him even when doing absurd things from people's point of view."

Some scholars describe the ultimate truth in terms of *presence*, some others describe it in terms of *nothingness*, and some in terms of *absence*.

A *self-realized* person does not get caught in these debates because he realizes the formless existence as his *real self* in a doubtless manner, and he does not need to rely on theories as such about the ultimate truth.

Due to the force of his remaining destined karma though, his body may sometimes do things which are absurd or childish from other people's point of view; but since he himself remains free of the *sense of doer-ship*, therefore, in reality, he does not become the doer of those absurd things.

(Note: In non-dualism, the ultimate truth gets described in terms of *existence*, which, by default, implies *a certain presence.*

This verse does not deny the presence of that existence, but it only indicates the *lack of interest* on part of a *self-realized* person *to describe the truth using words.*)

Verse 18.20

"No insistence by the *courageous person*, either in *activity* or in *inactivity*,
As and when things come, by doing them, he stays happily."

Those who seek pleasures, insist on activity; and those who seek liberation, insist on withdrawal from activity.

A *self-realized* person, however, does not seek either material prosperity or further spiritual progress, because he already stays at the pinnacle of it, on account of his *self-realization.*

Therefore, he does not need to push himself either towards *activity* or towards *inactivity.*

He just lets his remaining destined karma work itself out through his personality; sometimes by means of *activity* or sometimes by means of *inactivity*, but without any subjective insistence for it.

Verse 18.21

"Devoid of passions, devoid of dependency, moody and free of bondage,
Acts by the force of wind of the world, as if like a dry leaf."

An enlightened person leaves it to the destined karma to work itself out through his body, therefore, Ashtavakra portrays him as a dry leaf which gets flown by the wind, without any subjective interference from its side.

Verse 18.22

"For the *non-worldly person*, neither rejoice nor grief,
He, the *cool-minded*, always shines as if devoid of body."

A self-realized person realizes himself as the witnessing consciousness of psychology, and he does not blend with it as its subject.

Therefore, Ashtavakra calls him *cool-minded*.

His understanding remains doubtless and permanent; hence, he shines as if devoid of body.

Verse 18.23

"Neither abandonment anywhere nor hope also anywhere,
A *self-realized* person, courageous, *cool soul*."

Having realized the formless existence as his *real self*, a *self-realized* person no longer sees the need for abandonment, nor does he keep expectations in mind. Therefore, Ashtavakra calls him a *cool soul*.

Verse 18.24

"Quiet in nature and *zero-sum minded*, acts by the force of destiny,
For the courageous person, neither *pride* matters nor *humiliation*."

The concepts such as *pride* and *humiliation* are applicable to an individual who takes himself as the subject of psychology, due to his ignorance about the *real self*.
A *self-realized* person, on the other hand, realizes himself as the formless existence who never becomes the subject of psychology.
Therefore, he does not get affected by worldly concepts such as *pride* and *humiliation*.
The word *zero-sum minded* implies *lack of subjectivity* of a self-realized person.

Verse 18.25
"*Actions are done by the body and not by me – the pure consciousness*,
A person who thinks like this, does not do anything even while doing things."

A person who realizes himself as *pure consciousness* does not retain the sense of doer-ship, because he loses the subjectivity due to the realization.
His bodily activities take place on their own, by the force of remaining destined karma.

Verse 18.26
"He does activity without being assertive; like a child; does not get bothered even if it doesn't happen,
Such a liberated, *happy gentleman* shines, even while doing activity in the world."

Just like a child does activity without being worried about its results, a self-realized person also does that way; and that too, due to the force of his remaining destined karma.

Some of his actions may produce great results or some of his actions may not produce anything worthy. He neither gets excited nor dismayed by the end results of his actions.

Since he stays aloof from the results, Ashtavakra calls him a *happy gentleman*.

Verse 18.27

"Having listened to many opinions, a *courageous person* comes to an ultimate rest,

Neither imagines, nor knows, nor listens, nor sees."

In this verse, the term courageous person implies an enlightened person.

Different people try to state the ultimate truth in different ways.

Having listened to their debates and discussions, a courageous person finally stops getting involved in them. After that, when he realizes the ultimate truth within himself, and as his real self, he neither imagines about it, nor does he feel like knowing more about it theoretically.

Verse 18.28

"Due to the lack of meditation and distraction, he is neither liberation-seeker nor otherwise,

Convinced, seeing as imaginary, that *great person* is the all-pervasive existence itself."

In this verse, the term *great person* implies an *enlightened person*.

Having realized the all-pervasive existence as his *real self*, he neither remains a spiritual seeker nor does he remain otherwise.

He neither gets distracted nor does he need to meditate.

He realizes that the world is an illusory appearance, and his *real self* is the formless existence, which is the only reality.

Verse 18.29

"Inside whom the ego is there, he *does not*, but still *does*,
By the *ego-less courageous person*, *not done* is really *not done*."

The concept in the intellect of an ignorant person that *I am this individual subject* gives rise to the ego. Such a person keeps a strong sense of doer-ship and he can only think in terms of *doing* and *not doing*. For *doing*, he is required to make an effort. To keep quiet also, an effort is needed on his part. Hence, his *not doing* is also a form of *doing*.

On the contrary, a *self-realized* person – whose ego has subsided along with the sense of doer-ship – does not consider himself to be the doer, as he remains aware of the fact that the actions are happening by the force of destined karma. Established in the understanding of the *real self*, he becomes quiet by his very nature due to the loss of subjectivity.

Therefore, his *not doing* does not require any efforts like in the case of an ignorant person.

Verse 18.30

"Neither turbulent nor satisfied, nor does a thing, devoid of vibrations,
Devoid of expectations, with doubts dispelled, the mind of a liberated person shines."

A liberated person realizes himself as *pure consciousness* who, in its reality, never becomes the subject of psychology.

Therefore, he does not take himself as a subject of mental turbulence or vibrations. He realizes beyond doubt that his *real self* is the formless existence. His purity of heart, and clarity of understanding, becomes the light of his conscience. Hence, Ashtavakra describes him as a person with a *shining mind.*

Verse 18.31

"Neither for meditation nor for actions too, whose mind moves,
But without a cause, he meditates and does."

With his realization of the *real self*, a liberated person already stays at the pinnacle of spiritual progress.

He does not need meditation because he realizes the ever-peaceful nature of his being.

He does not take himself as the doer of activity as he understands that the actions happen due to the force of destined karma.

Due to the force of destined karma though, he might be seen either meditating at times or doing an activity, but even then, he remains without any personal cause due to the *loss of subjectivity* that occurs with *self-realization.*

Verse 18.32

"Having listened to the truth, an unwise person becomes clueless,
Even an intelligent person imports hesitation like the unwise."

An ignorant person with an impure mind and not enough clarity of thoughts, may become clueless having listened to this wisdom because of his strong sense of individuality and strong sense of doer-ship.

On the other hand, an intelligent person who has understood the truth well, may sometimes behave like a clueless ignorant person, because of the force of his remaining destined karma.

The destined karma works itself out by dominating the intellect first, and then getting the action done through the body.

It can have three forces pushing it:

1. Strong force. 2. Medium force. 3. Weak force.

In the case of an ignorant person, the destined karma pushed by all three forces dominate the intellect.

In the case of an enlightened person, only the portion pushed by the *strong force* dominates the intellect.

Therefore, he may appear to behave like a clueless ignorant person, but only sometimes.

Verse 18.33

"The *concentration* and *restraint* are practiced by an unwise person,
A *brave one* who stays as if *dormant* in his own *self*, does not see a purpose with them."

During the waking state, the *senses*, the *mind* and the *prana* (air within the body) remain functional.

During the dream state, the *mind* and the *prana* remain functional.

During deep sleep, only the *prana* remains functional.

The *concentration* and *restraint* are the practices which can be practiced only during waking state.

These practices are performed by an individual subject who sees meaning and purpose in the waking state world.

A *self-realized* person does not see meaning and purpose in the waking state world, because he understands the illusory nature of it.

He also realizes that his *real self* remains ever present as the *existential foundation* for the three states; and not as the subject of them.

Therefore, due to the *lack of subjectivity* on his part, he remains as if *dormant* during the waking state.

Doubt: But in the case of a *self-realized* person also, the mind and the senses remain functional during the waking state. So, how can he remain *dormant* in the waking state?

Answer: In this verse, dormancy implies staying aloof from the developments of the waking state world due to the lack of subjectivity for it.

This kind of *dormancy* becomes possible with the realization of the *real self*, who remains present as the *witnessing consciousness* for the mental transitions while the mind transits between waking, dreaming and deep sleep states.

Verse 18.34

"Either from *efforts* or from *non-efforts*, an unwise person does not find contentment,
By the mere conviction of truth, an intelligent person becomes content."

In the case of an ignorant person, *efforts* and *non-efforts* are like the two sides of the same coin, because the sense of doer-ship remains strong in him in both the situations.

In the case of an intelligent person, contentment comes on its own merely by the realization that he is not the doer/enjoyer subject.

Verse 18.35

"*Pure, conscious, lovely, complete, devoid of duality* and *free of contamination*;

People who are inclined towards practice, don't understand the *self* like this."

Ignorant people – who take themselves as *individual selves* – get engaged in activity-based practices in order to realize the *real self*.

The noteworthy fact is that the *real self* remains present as the very *being* of the practitioner even before the practitioner begins the practice.

The real self is an eternal existence who remains ever present as the witness of all practices. He remains so before the practice begins, during the practice and even after the practice is over.

The *self-realization* is a journey of understanding, and it is not a material process. Also, the *understanding* is a non-material effect. The very nature of the *real self* is *consciousness*; therefore, it cannot be realized by means of a practice involving material transformations.

It can only be realized by shifting our attention from objectifiable appearances to the existential reality of our *being*.

Verse 18.36

"Do not attain liberation, the unwise people, by an *activity-based practice*,

Blessed is a person who, by mere knowledge, stays free and without activity."

Ignorant people get engaged in active practices to attain liberation, because they believe that liberation is a metaphysical effect that can be created by means of either production, transformation or refinement activity.

They do not understand that such an effect would be temporary only; and, by definition, *liberation* cannot be temporary.

An intelligent person, on the other hand, who understands this, simply shifts his attention from *the activity-based practices of the objective world* to *the existential reality of his being*, and thereby, gets liberated.

This *liberation* remains permanent because the *existential reality of our being* is an omnipresent existence that eternally remains present as the foundation of the *subject*, of the *object* and of the relationship between the two.

Interestingly, only a rare person understands this mystery, therefore, Ashtavakra calls him *a blessed one.*

Verse 18.37

"An unwise person, who wants to *become* it, does not attain the *absolute existence*,
Unwillingly also, a brave person remains as the *absolute existence.*"

An unwise person who thinks that *he is an individual subject of the phenomenal world*, tries to become the *all-pervasive existence* through activity-based spiritual practices.

He remains far from knowing the reality because he approaches the reality by holding on to the idea that *he is an individual subject.*

On the other hand, a wise person, who understands that the *absolute existence is his real self*, always remains as that, willingly or unwillingly.

Doubt: How can one become and remain as the *absolute existence* without his own will?

Answer: The working of knowledge does not depend upon the will of an individual subject.

Heat is the very nature of fire, and whoever puts his hand into it will get burnt regardless of his willingness or unwillingness.

Similarly, knowledge does not require the willingness of a subject to do its job.

Once knowledge brings *self-realization*, the previously held idea that *I am an individual subject* vanishes; and then remains the *absolute existence*, which is our real *being*.

This *being* always remains as it is because it never becomes the subject of phenomenal experiences.

Verse 18.38

"Unwise people, busy with their baseless *insistence*, strengthen the worldly tendencies;

But the very root of this disguising world is uprooted by the wise people."

Although insistence can be of any kind, but, in the context of our subject matter, we can say that Ashtavakra uses the word insistence to imply certain beliefs that guide an ignorant person's behavior vis-a-vis his religious or spiritual practices.

These beliefs are of two kinds: 1. Ritualistic belief. 2. Superstition.

They are based on the presence of a certain cause-effect relationship formed by the mind.

Those who get engaged in ritualistic practices tend to insist upon their beliefs that are related with the rituals.

Other commoners tend to have belief in the form of superstition.

In both cases, ignorance of these people is obvious, as they tend to ignore their real self who exists beyond all cause-effect relationships.

These people also tend to take the cause-effect relationship as a reality because they do not understand the illusory nature of the phenomenal world.

On the other hand, a wise person, who knows that his *real self* is an unqualified formless existence, uproots the very cause of individuality - and the subsequent belief system too - from his intellect.

Therefore, he does not remain *insistent* any longer.

Verse 18.39

"An unwise person does not get peace even when he craves for *pacification*,
A courageous person, with conviction, always remains peaceful."

An unwise person carries *ignorance* in the intellect and considers himself as an individual subject. Then he tries to pacify the mind to get some peace; but it does not bring permanent peace to him because as long as the subjectivity remains present, the peace cannot last.

A wise person, due to his self-realization, gets convinced that he is that existence which remains eternally peaceful because it never becomes the subject of phenomenal experiences.

Verse 18.40

"Where is *self-realization* for him who remains occupied by the *seen* objects?
Courageous people do not see them; they see the indivisible *self*."

In this verse, the word Courageous people implies enlightened persons.

Doubt: Does it mean that a self-realized person does not perceive the objects?

Answer: Perception has two aspects:

Recognition of the physical dimensions and qualities of objects.

Knowing them to be either as reality or unreality.

An enlightened person recognizes the seen objects as physical objects along with their dimensions and qualities, however, he does not take them as reality, because he understands their illusory nature; like the objects in a dream.

Verse 18.41

"Where is the *restraint* for an unwise person who forcibly shuts the mind?
A brave person, who rests peacefully in himself, always has a *natural restraint.*"

An unwise person tries to restrain the mind by trying to shut its functions down by means of practice; but his effort remains based on ignorance that makes him believe that *he is an individual subject who is doing the practice.*

Therefore, the root of the problem remains with him, and the effort he makes goes in vain.

A wise person, on the other hand, by getting rid of the false sense of individuality, removes the very root of the problem, and thereby becomes eternally peaceful.

Verse 18.42

"Some person takes it as *reality*, some as *unreality*,
Devoid of both, just as it is, remains un-anxious."

Oftentimes spiritual philosophers debate about the reality or unreality of the material world, but they remain undecided because their debate remains confined to the realm of words which can only function using *mental constructs*; and a mental construct can be deceptive if it is used without the support of evidence.

An enlightened person, having understood the formless existence as his *real self*, doesn't depend on the *perceptual judgments* regarding the world.

His doubts vanish due to his realization, his mind ceases, and he remains content in his *real self*.

Doubt: Does it mean that a *self-realized* person becomes *agnostic* in some ways?

Answer: No. On the contrary, he becomes convinced about the nature of his *real self*, and that of the material world too.

If we go by impersonal scriptural evidence such as *Upanishad*, then we can get convinced that *the material world is an illusion.*

We can use logical evidence too, but it should be used to decipher the *scriptural evidence.*

If we use *logic* alone, then it can be deceptive and may not help us arrive at a conclusion.

Verse 18.43

"Unwise people try to get the feel of the *pure non-dual self*,
Failing to understand, due to an illusory spell, they remain
attached to the world till they remain alive."

The feelings operate only within the realm of psychology; whereas *self-realization* stays in the realm of understanding.

Our *real self - the non-dual and all-pervasive existence* - cannot become an object of psychological experience.

It cannot become an object of intellectual understanding either.

All efforts, therefore, to experience it through mental or intellectual experience will only go in vain.

The unwise people, who do not understand this reality of the *self*, keep trying to realize it through the mental or psychological experiences, applying emotions or feelings. As a result, they fail to realize it.

Doubt: An individual only has mental and intellectual means available to him. If he cannot realize the *real self* through the mental or intellectual means, then he can never realize the *real self*.

Answer: To address this, we first need to understand the nature of *self-realization*:

To begin with, the *real self* is not a totally unknown entity for us. We know that we exist. Hence, we have a partial realization already. Now the only thing which is required for us is to take our understanding to its completion. It can be done by simply removing the doubts about the nature of the *real self*. Once the doubts are removed, then we would realize that our *being* was always the *real self*; and it was never an individual form. It was our *ignorance* that made us believe that our being is an individual subject.

Doubt: But removal of doubts is an intellectual process.

Answer: Removal of doubts is an intellectual process for sure, but that does not mean that we can grasp the *real self* as an object of perception.

The real self gets realized subjectively – as *our own self*, in terms of *I am that*. This realization is deeper than the intellectual process. The intellectual and mental processes can function due to the existential foundation of the *real self*.

In short, the *real self* is an eternal existence which serves as the foundation for the *subjects* and for the *objects* too; and it does not become an object in itself.

Since the existence is omnipresent and self-evident, therefore the realization of it dawns on its own when the doubts get removed from the intellect.

Verse 18.44

"The intellect of a *liberation-seeker* does not stay without *objective dependency*;
Devoid of *objective dependency*, desire-less, stays the intellect of a liberated person."

A person who takes himself as an *individual self*, and thinks that he can attain liberation by remaining as an *individual subject*, engages himself in external means.

His intellect, therefore, remains occupied with different notions, theories and ideas.

He thinks of spiritual means only in terms of *subject-object relationships*; therefore, he continues to carry *objective dependency* in his intellect.

On the other hand, a person who realizes that the *real self* is the foundation of the *subject-object relationship* and it never becomes the subject of transactional affairs, drops the *objective dependency* from his intellect.

Verse 18.45 & Verse 18.46

"Seeing enticements as lions, surprised *refugees* try hard to embrace concentration and restraint;
But seeing a desire-less peaceful lion, the enticements themselves run away; not strong enough, they serve and appease him."

In the first verse above, the word refugees implies spiritual seekers who want to forcibly practice the restraint of mental functions.

These kinds of spiritual seekers see enticements as a danger to their practice of concentration and meditation. They want to run away to a place where they will not have to encounter the enticements of the world.

However, they do not understand that the worldly enticements are not the root of the problem. The real problem lies in their thinking, which makes them take the world as a reality.

These kinds of spiritual seekers have multiple layers of ignorance. First, they think that *they are individual subjects.* Then they think that *the world is real and the enticements are real too.* They think that *they have to achieve liberation through an activity-based practice.* Therefore, whenever they see any possibility of encountering worldly enticements, they tend to react to it negatively, and they try to keep away from them.

An enlightened person, on the other hand, understands that the real problem neither lies in the world nor in the so-called enticements, but it lies in the wrong notion vis-ā-vis *the reality of the world* and vis-ā-vis *the sense of being an individual subject.*

He overcomes ignorance by discarding the wrong notion. After that, he does not feel it necessary to run away from the illusory world – and from the illusory enticements too – as he loses the sense of reality in them.

In the second verse above, this enlightened person is referred to as the *peaceful lion.*

Verse 18.47

"Does not hold on to the means of liberation, a *doubtlessly composed person,*

While seeing, listening, touching, smelling, enjoying and sitting, remains blissful."

In this verse, the term doubtlessly composed person implies a self-realized person.

He seldom loses his composure due to an assurance that he receives in his intellect sourced from his understanding of the real self. He realizes that the real self is not an objective target that can be achieved through external means; because the real self is an omnipresent existence and that is his real being.

Therefore, he remains blissful while doing all his routine activities.

Verse 18.48

"By merely listening about the reality, an un-anxious person with a pure intellect,
Does not see the *Do's*, the *Don'ts* and the *apathy*."

Knowledge works instantly on a person who has a pure mind and a sharp intellect. As soon as he hears the wisdom about the *real self*, he realizes himself as the eternal and formless being.

After that he does not see any real meaning in the prescriptions of the *Do's* and *Don'ts* because he does not hanker after worldly objectives any longer.

Verse 18.49

"Whenever something comes, then he does that, the modest one,
Auspicious or *inauspicious*, his behavior appears as that of a child."

A self-realized person remains non-insistent.

He simply observes his destined karma being worked out through his body; therefore, this verse describes him as the modest one.

He goes beyond the concepts of *auspicious* and *inauspicious*. Hence, his behavior becomes as innocent as that of a child.

Verse 18.50

"From freedom comes the happiness, from freedom comes the attainment of the *ultimate*,
From freedom goes the *refrain*, from freedom comes the attainment of the *supreme post*."

The unqualified existence remains permanently free because it is *the only reality*, and because it never becomes the subject of the phenomenal world.

Freedom comes when a person realizes the unqualified existence as his real self.

A wise person does realize it that way, and enjoys real freedom. He becomes as if an idol of the *supreme post*, the *ultimate truth*, which is that existence itself.

Doubt: But we still see a knowledgeable person bound by the laws of nature and behaving according to prevailing social customs.

Answer: As outsiders, we can only see the body of a knowledgeable person, which has a certain destined karma to be worked out.

Hence, the knowledgeable person may appear to be bound by the laws of nature or he may appear behaving according to the prevailing social customs; however, in his own *understanding*, the *sense of being an individual self* doesn't remain true any longer.

This *understanding* is not a material, therefore, it cannot be judged or commented upon from outside.

This understanding is unique because it merges the knowledge and the experience together. Then it becomes a realization.

After that, the body continues to function till the remaining destined karma of the current life gets worked out completely; and till that happens, other people can see the body of the knowledgeable person functioning just as before.

Verse 18.51

"When the *non-doer-ship* and the *non-enjoyer-ship* of the *real self* gets acknowledged,
Then surely subside the tendencies of the mind."

The *real self* is the existential foundation of the time-space phenomenon; and it never becomes the subject of it.

Therefore, it never becomes the doer of activities nor does it become the enjoyer of experiences.

With this realization, the tendencies of the mind subside, in the sense that *the 'I' gets separated from the tendencies of the mind.*

The *self* gets realized as a *seer*, and the *tendencies of the mind* become a part of the *seen phenomenon.*

Verse 18.52

"Even if *flamboyant* or *inactive*, the *state* of a *courageous person* shines,
And not the artificial peace of an unwise person who has desires in his mind."

In this verse, the term courageous person implies an enlightened person.

He shines in all his behavior, whether flamboyant or inactive; because of the *lack of subjectivity* on his part towards that behavior and its result.

On the other hand, an unwise person who takes himself as *the individual subject of activity*, remains deluded even when he tries to pacify his mind through artificial techniques.

Verse 18.53

"They may enjoy great indulgences or may stay in the mountain caves.
Devoid of imagination, the *courageous persons* remain unbound and free in their intellect."

Since a *self-realized* person does not see the world and its experiences as a reality, therefore he remains as comfortable in worldly indulgences as he does in deserted places like mountain caves.

Neither does he give importance to his worldly position nor does he remain bound by the concepts such as status and authority.

He remains unbound and free in his intellect.

Verse 18.54

"Seeing a scholar, a deity, a holy place, a woman, a king and a dear one,
A courageous person greets them with respect but without any desire in the heart."

In the absence of worldly purpose, a *self-realized* person does not approach or greet anybody with any ulterior motives in his mind. He may greet different kinds of people as a matter of formality when he happens to encounter them when walking through the streets, parks, public places or elsewhere, but he does not see any purpose with them or expects any favors from them.

Verse 18.55

"By *servants, sons, wives, grandsons, relatives*; laughed at or condemned,
A wise person does not incur any perversion in his mind."

Since a wise person does not keep the sense of reality into the affairs of the world, therefore he does not get perturbed by the reactions he gets from others.

At times, his closed ones may laugh at him or they may condemn him, but that leaves no effect on him as he understands the fact that those who are laughing at him or condemning him are bound by worldly concepts; and those worldly concepts have shaped their attitude.

Since he himself does not remain bound by those attitudes formed by the worldly concepts, therefore he does not get perturbed by them.

Verse 18.56

"Satisfied yet not satisfied, disappointed yet not disappointed.
The amazing state of his can only be understood by the ones who are like him."

Satisfaction and disappointment – are psychological conditions.

A wise person realizes himself to be the witness of psychology, therefore he does not intervene in the psychological affairs subjectively.

His psychological tendencies manifest due to his remaining destined karma; but internally he realizes himself as the witness of the psychological tendencies.

Sometimes he may appear to be satisfied, or sometimes he may appear to be disappointed, but internally he remains in his own bliss.

Verse 18.57

"*Duty-boundness* is the world; wise persons do not see that,
They remain *zero-sum minded, formless, devoid of perversion, devoid of impurities.*"

The sense of *duty-boundness* comes when we see purpose in the world. We see purpose in the world because:

We take it as a reality

We take ourselves as *individual subjects* of it

On account of loss of purpose due to their *self-realization*, the enlightened beings do not see themselves as duty-bound individuals.

They do not remain tied to an individual mind any longer, hence, Ashtavakra calls them *zero-sum minded.*

They understand themselves as the unqualified existence, hence, they remain formless in their essence.

They do not get attached to psychology; therefore, they remain devoid of perversion and impurities.

Verse 18.58

"Even while not doing anything, due to excitement, an unwise person remains busy everywhere.
While doing many things also, a wise person does not become anxious."

Even when idle, an unwise person remains busy in his mind because he takes himself as the subject of psychology.

On the other hand, a wise person – on account of his lack of subjectivity towards the mind – remains free even while performing actions.

Verse 18.59

"Sits blissfully, sleeps blissfully, comes and goes blissfully,
Talks blissfully, eats blissfully, in routine life as well; a cool person."

The omnipresent existence is the source of all bliss.

Its presence is the cause of the sense *of being existent* in all creatures.

Since an enlightened person realizes himself as the existence, he remains blissful even while performing routine activities.

Verse 18.60

"Due to the very nature of whom, sorrows are not there, as is the case of other worldly people,
Calm as an ocean, devoid of misery, an enlightened person shines."

The *real self* is devoid of sorrow due to its very nature, because it never becomes the subject of phenomenal experiences.

An enlightened person, who realizes himself as that *real self*, becomes devoid of sorrows.

In the process of realization, his '*I*' gets separated from psychology. Hence, even when he does activity just as everyone else, he remains calm from within, like an ocean.

Verse 18.61

"*Non-activity* also, of an unwise person, becomes an *activity*.

Activity of a *courageous person* really gives the fruit of *non-activity*."

On account of his sense of doer-ship, an unwise person has to make an effort to remain non-active, since his mind pulls him in all directions.

On the other hand, a wise person remains free of the sense of doer-ship due to his realization.

Therefore, he enjoys the fruit of non-activity – the peace, even while among the activity.

Verse 18.62

"Dispassion is seen of an unwise person towards possessions.
But who has lost expectations from the body itself, for him,
where is the affection and where is the dispassion."

An ignorant person remains bound by the feelings of *Me* and *Mine*. He remains possessive of the things which belong to him. Therefore, when he becomes a *liberation-seeker*, he has to make an effort to disassociate himself from his possessions. This effort of his gives rise to a tendency known as *dispassion*.

On the other hand, for an enlightened person, who has given up his false sense of individuality, the possessions – or lack of them – does not remain an issue. He neither remains affectionate about them nor does he need to make an effort to remain dispassionate about them.

Verse 18.63

"Vision of an unwise person, always remains caught in (the
debate of) *being* and *non-being*.
For a wise person though, it really remains a *non-vision*."

An ignorant person who has not realized the *real self* tends to debate – and fluctuate – between the opinions of *being* and *non-being*, because he tries to understand the reality only at the level of intellect.

A wise person, on the other hand, actually realizes *the non-dual existence as his real self.* Therefore, he does not fluctuate between the opinions of *being* and *non-being*.

Philosophically speaking, the ultimate reality can be indicated as an *omnipresent being*.

The word *being* indicates *existence.*

The presence of an ultimate existence cannot be denied since the sense of *being existent* is a default sense that figures in automatically in every subject, object and perception.

Verse 18.64

"A wise person, like a child, remains desire-less in all the start-ups.
He does not remain glued to the actions even while doing them."

A child does most of its activities without worrying about their results. It simply gets driven by its instincts when it performs those activities.

An enlightened person also takes up activities without really worrying about their results.

It, however, does not mean that an enlightened person does the activities irresponsibly; but it only means that *he does not take himself as their subject and remains detached from their results.*

Verse 18.65

"Blessed is a *self-realized* person who remains indifferent in all situations.

His mind remains *devoid of craving* even while seeing,
listening, touching, smelling, eating and drinking."

Remaining indifferent in all situations comes naturally to an enlightened person because he realizes that the *real self* - the formless existence - remains indifferent in all situations due to its lack of subjectivity vis-a-vis those situations.

Therefore, he works out his remaining destined karma without craving for phenomenal experiences.

Verse 18.66

"Where is the *world*, and where is *its awareness*; where is the *goal* and where is *its means*,
For a wise person, who is like the *sky*, devoid of distractions."

An enlightened person realizes himself to be the formless and un-qualitative existence. Due to this realization, the concepts such as *goal and means* become irrelevant for him.

Only a person who takes himself as an *individual subject* needs to rely on thinking based on the concepts such as *goal and means*; not an enlightened person.

Verse 18.67

"The *monk* really conquers, a complete idol of joyous *self*,
His *state of being* remains natural and without any interruptions."

In this verse, the word *monk* implies *a self-realized person.*

The real joy is the *joy of being existent.*

The *monk* remains in eternal joy as he realizes that the source of all the joy is the formless existence, which is his *real self.*

Verse 18.68

"Why say more? The knower of truth,
Neither aspires for pleasures nor for liberation, always stays disinterested everywhere."

A knower of the truth realizes that his *real self* is the source of all happiness. Therefore, he neither aspires for material pleasures nor for spiritual liberation.

He remains disinterested due to the lack of attachment.

Verse 18.69

"The duality of the manifested elements is there for the sake of speech alone.
Having abandoned it, what duty remains for an enlightened person."

The duality of the manifested elements and the metaphysical concepts of ether etc. remain relevant for a person who is not aware of the fact that *he is pure consciousness existence.*

A wise person who realizes the *pure consciousness* as his *real self,* essentially transcends these metaphysical concepts.

Nothing remains to be sought in the physical world, from his perspective.

Verse 18.70

"Illusory is all this and nothing else, realizing like this, a convinced person,
Devoid of goal, becomes *non-intuitive, pure* and *quiet* by his very nature."

The world is an illusory phenomenon, and the formless existence is the reality.

With this conviction, an enlightened person does not feel a dire need to react to every single event that happens around him.

Therefore, in a way, he becomes *non-intuitive.*

This is a great strength which can be acquired only by disassociating the *'I'* from psychology.

It happens so in the case of an enlightened person due to his realization of the *real self.*

He becomes *pure* as he realizes the pure consciousness as his *real self.*

He becomes *quiet* due to the detachment that comes on account of his realization.

Verse 18.71

"He, who is an embodiment of *pure consciousness*, does not see the *seen phenomenon* as a reality,
For him where is *methodology*, where is *dispassion*, where is *renunciation* and where is *quietude.*"

From the highest standpoint of the *pure consciousness* – the *methodologies*, the concepts of *dispassion, renunciation* and *quietude* – do not have any relevance since they belong to the illusory phenomenon of the world.

For a wise person who realizes himself as the *pure consciousness*, these concepts become a part of the *seen* phenomenon, and they become redundant for him.

Verse 18.72

"Emanating by means of infinite forms, and not seeing the cosmos as a reality,
For him, where is the *bondage*, where is the *liberation*, where is the *joy* and where is the *grief.*"

Pure consciousness emanates through all the phenomenal forms because it is their *existential being*.

For a wise person who realizes himself as *pure consciousness*, the whole cosmos becomes an illusion.

Therefore, for him, the concepts such as *bondage, liberation, joy* and *grief* become redundant.

Verse 18.73

"Till the intellect remains active, an illusory world appears. Devoid of affection, devoid of ego and desire-less, shines a wise one."

Under the spell of ignorance, the intellect tends to attribute a false sense of reality to the world.

The intellect of a wise person, which has shed *ignorance*, does not keep the sense of reality vis-a-vis the phenomenal world.

Consequently, it also makes the enlightened person *ego-less* and *desire-less.*

Therefore, the enlightened person shines as against other ignorant people, like a pearl shines in the sand grains.

Verse 18.74

"*Permanent* and *devoid of anger*, like this the *self* is seen by a wise person,

For him, where is the knowledge, where is the universe, where is the body and where is the sense of *mine*."

The formless existence is our *real self*.

The real self is free of psychological reactions because it does not become the subject of psychology.

A wise person realizes himself as that permanent existence.

Due to this realization, the intellectual knowledge, the universe, the body and the sense of *'I'* or *'Mine'* – no longer matters to him.

Verse 18.75
"When an unwise seeker gives up the practice of restrain,
He starts imagining, talking nonsensically and assumes the
sense of doer-ship immediately."

Spiritual seekers can be divided into three categories:

Ordinary seekers: The seekers who have lots of impurities in their mind, and who cannot focus on any given topic for too long. Their mind gets swayed by desires too quickly, and they keep a strong sense of reality in the world.

Medium category seekers: The seekers who have some purity of mind, and have an intellect sharp enough to grasp the truth intellectually, but who need more contemplation on the spiritual wisdom to obtain the clarity.

Best category seekers: The seekers who have a very pure mind and a very sharp intellect. They understand the truth very quickly once they hear about it.

For the seekers of each of these categories, three different methods have been prescribed in the scriptures.

The *ordinary seekers* are supposed to purify their mind by means of service of Gurus, observation of restraint, and practice of austerities. After sufficient purification, they can listen to the scriptural wisdom. Then they need to reflect and contemplate on it, until they realize the truth.

The *better category seekers* are supposed to listen to the wisdom straight away, and then they are required to contemplate on it.

The *best category seekers* are only required to listen to the wisdom. They do not need further contemplation or reflection.

The above verse has been narrated for the first two categories of seekers, whose minds tend to get swayed due to desires.

Verse 18.76

"Having listened also, about the existence, an unwise person,
does not give up *ignorance.*
Externally he may become quiet for some time, but from within
he continues to seek pleasures."

In this verse, Ashtavakra uses the term *an unwise person* to point at a seeker who belongs to the *Better category.*

A *better category seeker* may have an intellectual appreciation of the spiritual wisdom, but he may not have enough conviction due to the want of further clarity and contemplation.

From within, he keeps seeking worldly pleasures so as to satisfy his psychological requirements, and he may tend to draw a false sense of happiness out of those pleasures.

Verse 18.77

"Whose passion for activity has subsided due to the knowledge,
while doing activity from people's point of view,
He does not get an occasion to act or speak."

It is the *ignorant mind* that binds us to karma due to the sense of reality it has in the world.

A wise person loses this sense of reality vis-a-vis the world, therefore, internally, his passion for activity subsides. Hence, even while he may be seen doing activities due to the force of destined karma, he still does not get bound by that activity as its subject.

Therefore, Ashtavakra says that a wise person does not really have an occasion to act or to speak.

Verse 18.78

"Where is the darkness, where is the light, where is the renunciation, where is anything at all,
For the *courageous person* who always remains devoid of distraction and trauma."

In this verse, Ashtavakra refers to an enlightened person as the *courageous person.*

For such a person, the duality of the world subsides effectively. Therefore, the concepts such as knowledge, ignorance and renunciation do not matter to him any longer. He becomes devoid of psychological distractions and traumas.

Verse 18.79

"Where is the *courageousness*, where is the *conscientiousness* and where is the fearlessness for an enlightened person,
Who is of indefinable nature and who is, in fact, devoid of nature."

An enlightened person becomes devoid of nature in the sense that he does not remain bound by the psychological tendencies.

For him, the qualities such as *courageousness, conscientiousness* and *fearlessness* become as illusory as any other aspect of the *seen phenomenon.*

Verse 18.80

"Neither heaven nor hell nor liberation either.
What more to say here? There remains nothing, from the realization standpoint."

The realms of heaven, hell and earthly life are relevant for an ignorant person who takes himself as an individual subject of the *seen phenomenon.*

The concept of liberation is relevant for the one who takes himself as a bound individual.

An enlightened person, on the other hand, realizes that he was never an individual subject but always the *pure consciousness.*

Therefore, for him, the realms of heaven, hell and earthly life become part of the illusory phenomenon.

Verse 18.81

"Neither prays for benefit, nor grieves by the lack of it.
Calm mind of a *courageous person* remains filled by the nectar alone."

The term courageous person implies an enlightened person.

An enlightened person attains the nectar of immortality on account of his self-realization.

He, therefore, doesn't pray for material benefits, nor does he grieve due to lack of them.

Verse 18.82

"Neither praises a calm person nor condemns a crooked person.
Indifferent to happiness and sorrow, he does not see any duties for himself."

In the absence of purpose in the affairs of the world, a *self-realized* person does not see a real requirement either to praise or to condemn anyone.

For him the psychological happiness and sorrows become the two sides of the same coin. Therefore, he remains indifferent to both of them.

Verse 18.83
"A *courageous person* neither hates the world nor craves to see the *real self*.
Free of joy and aversion, neither does he die nor does he live."

Due to the absence of the sense of reality in the world, an enlightened person does not feel the need to hate it. He does not have to make an activity-based effort for *self-realization* because he already realizes the formless existence as his *real self* and so also the illusory nature of such an effort.

His mind subsides. Therefore, he does not remain attached to the psychological tendencies of joy and aversion.

Verse 18.84
"Devoid of affection towards the progeny and wife, and devoid of desires in pleasures.
Devoid of worries about his own body and devoid of expectations, a wise person really shines."

An enlightened person - who realizes that the world is an illusory phenomenon - also realizes that his sons, wife and other individuals are part of the *seen* phenomenon.

He also realizes that it is the destined karma that is driving the body, and making it work in a certain way.

Hence, he does not seek to intervene psychologically into the affairs of his personality.

With this supreme understanding, he shines due to the *lack of subjectivity* on his part towards the *seen* objects.

Verse 18.85
"A wise person remains in peace everywhere, eats what comes in his plate,

Roams around willingly from place to place, sleeps wherever he is at the time of sunset."

Since he does not take the world as a reality, and remains content in his own understanding, he takes things as they come, and does not get affected by the prevailing social concepts such as status, prestige, etc.

Therefore, he remains ready to wander from place to place without any real purpose, and remains ready to sleep on the roadside during the wander.

He realizes himself to be the all-pervasive *consciousness*, therefore, remains peaceful everywhere.

Verse 18.86

"May the body fall or may it continue to work; it does not worry a great soul.
Forgetting about the *remaining* or *non-remaining* worldly life, he rests on the ground of his true nature."

An enlightened person realizes that his body will remain functional till the destined karma of the current life gets exhausted.

After that, it is bound to stop functioning, and will eventually fall somewhere.

Due to *self-realization,* he loses the sense of purpose in this illusory phenomenon of the world.

He attains eternal peace, and does not feel bothered about the *remaining* or *non-remaining* karma, because his *'I'* remains unassociated with the karmic play.

Verse 18.87

"*Impoverished, free roamer*, devoid of duality and doubt,

Unattached to objects, a wise person roams just like that."

A wise person may appear to work systematically or he may appear to be leading the life of a wandering monk. In either case, he remains free internally, due to his understanding of the *real self.*

Therefore, he may stay in one place or he may become a *free roamer*, he always remains unattached everywhere, in all conditions, since he realizes the illusory nature of the worldly dualities.

Verse 18.88

"*Unattached*, shines a *courageous person*, remains indifferent to the clay, rock and gold,

Having broken the *knot of the heart*, free of *Rajas* and *Tamas*."

The term *knot of the heart* can be interpreted in two ways:

Attachment, or

Misunderstanding about the *real self.*

They are two sides of the same coin – ignorance.

Ignorance is an effect that makes us take ourselves as something which we are not in reality.

Due to it, our mind sees meaning and purpose in this illusory world. That leads to the creation of attachments in the heart for worldly objects; but a wise person realizes himself as *pure consciousness*, therefore, he remains unattached; and since he does not see meaning in the world, he does not attach more value to the gold than that to the clay or rock.

Verse 18.89

"Inattentive everywhere and no desires in the heart,

With whom can the really satisfied free soul be compared with?"

Sometimes, an enlightened person may appear as if he is inattentive; but that happens due to his lack of interest in this mirage-like appearance called *the world.*

Also, he remains satisfied in his realization, not having to worry about fulfillment of desires; therefore, he cannot be compared with an ignorant individual who carries desires in his heart.

Verse 18.90

"Does not know while knowing, does not see while seeing,
Does not speak while speaking, who else is there like this,
except the desire-less wise person?"

An enlightened person understands himself to be the attribute-less existence, therefore he does not take himself as the subject of internal or external activity.

His personality functions just like that of any other individual, but the difference lies in their understanding.

The wise person realizes himself as the attribute-less existence, while others take themselves as individual subjects of the world.

Therefore, due to the lack of subjectivity, the wise person does not see even when his eyes are seeing, does not know even when his mind is knowing, does not speak even when his tongue is speaking.

Verse 18.91

"Be a beggar or a king, the desire-less person really shines,
Whose intellect has lost meaning in the feelings of good and bad."

Having feelings is one thing, and attaching meaning to them is another. When we attach meaning to the feelings, the *'I'* gets involved in the process, and then we get affected by those chemical patterns of feelings.

A wise person understands that the so-called individual *'I'* need not become the subject of those feelings.

Hence, he does not attach too much meaning to his feelings as he realizes himself to be the witness of the feelings, and not as party to them.

Therefore, irrespective of his worldly status, he shines because of *self-realization.*

Verse 18.92

"Where is the *free-spiritedness*, where is the *hesitation* or where is the *conviction*,
For the wise person who is an embodiment of openness and solemnity."

Free-spiritedness and *hesitation* are psychological tendencies. Sometimes, the conviction can also remain only at an intellectual level.

These tendencies cannot portray an enlightened person correctly as he does not remain bound by these tendencies as their subject.

On the contrary, he always stays assured because he realizes himself as *pure consciousness.* He does not pose or pretend externally to extract worldly benefit. Hence, in a way, he becomes an embodiment of openness and solemnity.

Verse 18.93

"An enlightened person who is devoid of hope and miseries,

The Inner experience enjoyed by him, how and to whom can it be told?"

The inner experience of an enlightened person is not a mental experience. It is an understanding of the *oneness* in which the sense of duality subsides totally. There the mind also subsides to an extent because the doubts, efforts, and external measures vanish. The *knower* and the *known* become one as the dependency on the subject-object relationship ends. This is clearly not a matter of a verbal description since the affair of speech remains bound by the limitations of words which can only describe an objective experience.

The experience of *self-realization* is not an objective experience, but it is an experience wherein the knowledge tends to unite with the experience of *being existent*.

In objective experience, *the object of experience, the person as an experiencer* and *the phenomenon of experience* remain separate from each other.

In *self-realization*, the *triad* gets dissolved; not physically or mechanically, but on account of the loss of the false sense of *'I'*.

Verse 18.94

"*Sleeps not* even while sleeping, *dreams not* even while dreaming,
Does not remain awake even while awake; A *courageous person* remains satisfied in every state."

The mental states such as deep sleep, dream and waking are the states through which the mind transits every day.

An ignorant person identifies himself with the mind, therefore, he thinks that it is his *being* that transits through these states.

On the other hand, an enlightened person realizes himself as *pure consciousness*, therefore, he does not identify himself with these mental states, nor does he take himself as the subject of them.

From a counter perspective, the personality of an enlightened person might be seen transiting through these states, but from his own perspective, he neither wakes, nor dreams nor sleeps, because he does not take himself to be the subject of the transitions of mind.

Verse 18.95

"A wise person worries yet worries not, has senses yet remains devoid of them,
Intelligent yet dumb, has ego yet devoid of it."

From other people's point of view, and due to his remaining destined karma, the personality of an enlightened person might be seen exhibiting the tendency of worry, or might be seen doing routine work involving senses; but internally he realizes himself as the formless existence which does not have the subjectivity vis-a-vis the personality.

Due to his past habits, he might be seen indulging in some intelligent work or at times he might be taken as a proud person, but internally, he remains free of all psychological contaminations on account of his realization of the *real self*.

Verse 18.96

"Neither happy nor sorrowful, neither renunciate nor attached,
Neither seeks liberation nor liberated, neither *anything* nor *not anything*."

An enlightened person remains free of the psychological duel of happiness and sorrows. He neither identifies himself with renunciation nor does he seek company of worldly people.

He remains content in his own *being*, so much so that he does not seek liberation nor does he need to prove himself as the liberated one.

He neither identifies with anything worldly nor does he take pride in it, nor does remain averse to it.

All these dualities matter to an ignorant individual, not to a *self-realized* person.

Verse 18.97

"In distraction also not distracted, in meditation also not meditative,
Not inert in inertia, a wise person, not scholarly in wisdom too."

From outside, a wise person may appear to show different behavioral patterns. He may appear distracted, meditative, inert or scholarly; but internally he does not remain involved in any of these, due to the lack of subjectivity vis-a-vis the mind on account of his *self-realization.*

Verse 18.98

"A liberated person remains fine in all conditions, free from the sense of being duty-bound,
Remains indifferent everywhere due to lack of desire, does not remember his past action or inaction."

A liberated person simply does activities due to the force of destined karma, and does not consider himself to be the subject of them or of their results. He does not need to remember those actions performed by his personality, just as we do not need to remember the dream activities performed by our dream persona.

Verse 18.99

"Neither gets pleased when praised nor gets annoyed when criticized,

Neither grieves over death nor congratulates life."

Ignorant individuals who consider themselves as *individual subjects*, worry about praise, criticism, life and death.

A wise person, on the other hand, remains free of that sense, hence there remains nobody in there as a subject, to worry about praise, criticism, life or death.

Verse 18.100

"Neither chases the crowd nor flees to the forest,

Wherever and however a wise person stays, he remains indifferent."

Everywhere and in all conditions, a wise person remains indifferent because he realizes the illusory nature of the phenomenal world.

He does not take himself as an individual subject, therefore he does not bother about the *pairs of opposites* that the phenomenal world offers to him at the psychological and physical level.

Chapter 19

Verse 19.1

Janaka said,

"Having received the wisdom; From the heart,

Different types of *thorns of doubts* have been thrown out by me."

In this verse, the word *heart* implies *intellect*, since the doubts reside in the intellect.

Those doubts have been cleared by the understanding given by Ashtavakra.

Janaka equates the doubts with thorns because the *doubts about the real self* become the cause of suffering.

Verse 19.2

"Where is the *ritual* and where is the *desire*, where is the *wealth* and where is the *conscientiousness*,

Where is the *duality* or where is the *non-duality* for me, who remains situated in my own glory."

Janaka became devoid of desires due to *self-realization*.

In the absence of desires, he no longer remained concerned about *rituals* or *conscientiousness*. The talk of *duality* and *non-duality* also became meaningless to him since he actually realized himself as an unqualified existence.

Verse 19.3

"Where is the past or where is the future or where is the present either,
Where is the space for me, who remains situated in my own glory."

The ideas of past, present and future are related with the idea of time; and the idea of time is created by the mind when it notices movement of objects around it. Then it divides the events in terms of past, present and future.

Similarly, the mind creates the factor of space when it wants to know the dimensions of an object.

The time-space factors matter to a person who considers himself as the individual subject of the time-space phenomenon.

Janaka realized himself as an attribute-less existence.

He realized that the time-space phenomenon is an illusion, therefore he could see the frame of time-space – and the events taking place in it – as a dream.

Verse 19.4

"Where is the *self* and where is the *non-self*, where is the *auspicious* and where is the *inauspicious* likewise;
Where is the worry or where is the lack of it, for me who remains situated in my own glory."

The talks of *self* or *non-self* no longer remained enchanting for Janaka, because he realized that the *real self* is a formless omnipresent existence.

For him the *pairs of opposite* such as *auspicious and inauspicious* also became irrelevant. He no longer remained apprehensive about his future, therefore, the psychological factors such as worry etc. became ineffective for him from his own perspective.

Verse 19.5

"Where is the dream state and where is the deep sleep, where is the waking state likewise,
Where is the *fourth one* and where is the fear for me, who remains situated in my own glory."

The waking, dreaming and deep sleep are the states of mind because it is the mind that transits through these states.

Some people consider the *fourth one* also as a mental state which they call *Turiya* or *Samadhi.*

Janaka, however, realizes that the *fourth one* is *not* a mental state, but it is the very existence, which remains present in – and beyond – the earlier three states.

Therefore, the term *fourth* is a fictitious number; a term which is used only to distinguish it from the three mental states.

The *real self* as the *fourth one* always remains present as the foundation of the three mental states, and although it does not become the subject of mental transitions, but it appears to have become so, due to *ignorance.*

With the proper knowledge of the *real self*, the *ignorance* gets dispelled, and along with it, the *apparent subjectivity* towards the three states also ends.

This *end of subjectivity* is called *Moksha* or *liberation* in spiritual parlance, because it ensures permanent freedom from suffering.

Verse 19.6

"Where is the *far* and where is the *near*, where is the *external* and where is the *internal,*
Where is the *gross* and where is the *subtle,* for me who remains situated in my own glory."

The spatial factors such as *far* and *near*, the spatial distinction such as *external* and *internal*, and the dimensional measures such as *gross* and *fine* remain relevant for an individual who considers himself to be the subject of the *time-space phenomenon.*

Janaka, on the other hand, realized himself to be the formless existence who never becomes the subject of the time-space phenomenon; therefore, the spatial and dimensional factors became meaningless to him from his own perspective.

Verse 19.7

"Where is the death and where is the life, where is the world and where is the worldly,
Where is the dissolution and where is the meditation, for me who remains situated in my own glory."

When a subtle body leaves the gross body, it is called death.

When the subtle body gets a new gross body, it is called life.

Janaka realized himself as the formless existence which is an immortal *being*, therefore, he no longer took himself as an individual persona composed of the combination of gross and subtle body.

Subsequently, the concepts of birth and death became irrelevant for him from his own perspective, just as the idea of spiritual practices.

Verse 19.8

"Enough of the talks of *three means*, enough of the talks of yoga,
Enough of the talks of *knowledge*, for me who remains situated in my own glory."

In this verse, the term *three means* imply:

1.*Performance of rituals*
2.*Earning money*
3.*Fulfillment of desires.*

Janaka had already accomplished the *fourth means* - the *liberation* - due to his realization of *oneness.*

Therefore, he no longer remained interested in the religious talks about the earlier three means.

For the same reason, he no longer remained interested in the practice-based methodologies such as *yoga.*

He became an embodiment of the ultimate reality due to his realization.

Chapter 20

Verse 20.1

Janaka said,

"Where are the *metaphysical elements* and where is the body,
where are the senses and where is the mind,
Where is the *absence* and where is the disappointment, in my
spotless *self*."

Janaka realized the illusory nature of the *metaphysical elements* which apparently compose the phenomenal world.

The term *absence* became meaningless to him because he realized that the *seen* phenomenon is filled by the formless existence; and that formless existence is an omnipresent being.

The psychological factors such as disappointment lost their power over him since he no longer mistook himself as the subject of psychology.

Verse 20.2

"Where are the *scriptures*, where is the *knowledge of the self*
and where is the *empty mind* too,
Where is the *satisfaction* and where is the *desireless-ness*, for
me whose sense of duality has subsided."

The topics such as *scriptures, knowledge of the self, empty mind, satisfaction and desireless-ness* remain relevant for an ignorant individual; but, for Janaka, these topics became a part of the illusory phenomenon due to his realization.

Verse 20.3

"Where is the *wisdom*, where is the *ignorance*, where is the *'I'*, where is *this* and where is the *mine*,
Where is the *bondage*, where is the *liberation*, and where is the *form*, for my formless *real self*."

The topics such as bondage and liberation also became dream topics for him after the realization of the *real self*.

The duel of *this* and *that* vanished because he realized himself to be the all-pervasive existence.

In the absence of an individual *'I'*, the possessive tendency such as *mine*, also vanished.

Verse 20.4

"Where is the destined karma and where is the *pre-death liberation*,
Where is the *post-death liberation* too, for the eternally formless *being*."

The destined karma or the ideas of *pre-death/post-death liberation* became part of the dream for him since he realized himself as the eternal and formless existence.

Verse 20.5

"Where is the *doer*, where is the *enjoyer* and where is the *passive intuition* too,
Where is the *direct knowledge* and where is the fruit of it, for me who remains devoid of subjectivity."

The formless existence is eternal, and it never becomes the subject of phenomenal activity, either as the doer or as the enjoyer.

Janaka no longer identifies himself as the subject of passive intuition and knowledge too, because they involve mental and intellectual activity.

Verse 20.6

"Where is the world, where is the *liberation-seeker*, where is the *yogi* and where is the *wise person*,
Where is the *bound person* and where is the *liberated one*, in my *non-dual self*."

Gone is the dream where Janaka used to identify himself with an individual persona who was seeking liberation.

The idea of being present in the world as an individual subject, the idea of liberation, the idea of being a yogi or the idea of being a wise person, became irrelevant for him, now that he realized himself to be the non-dual existence.

Verse 20.7

"Where is the creation, where is the destruction too, where is the goal and where is the *means*,
Where is the practitioner and where is the perfection, in my *non-dual self*."

The idea of creation and destruction of the world matters to a person who wants to continue with the world as its subject.

Similarly, the terms *goal* and *means* also matter to the one who wants to achieve worldly pleasures.

Janaka realized himself as the *non-dual existence*. Hence, these ideas became irrelevant for him, from his own perspective.

Verse 20.8

"Where is the *protagonist*, where is the *evidence* and where is the *conviction* too,
Where is the *something* or where is the *nothing*, for the pure *me*."

During scholarly debates, when an individual tries to convince others, he – as the protagonist – needs to present certain evidence to them in order to convince them about his point of view.

The debates matter to a person only as long as he considers himself as an individual subject.

For Janaka, the apparent duality vanished with his realization. Therefore, he was no longer interested in becoming a protagonist of a certain point of view; neither did he need to present the evidence to others, nor did he need to assert his own conviction about the truth.

He became satisfied with his realization. Therefore, the tendency of the mind to reach out to the world did not matter to him any longer.

Verse 20.9

"Where is the distraction and where is the concentration, where is the dumbness and where is the stupidity,
Where is the joy and where is the grief, for the always inactive *me*."

Distraction, concentration, dumbness, stupidity, joy, and grief are the psychological notions which take shape when a person remains active in the world carrying the sense of doer-ship in his mind.

Janaka, on account of his *self-realization*, lost that sense of doer-ship, therefore, he remained as good as inactive from his own point of view, while the individual named Janaka could still be seen as an active person by other people.

Verse 20.10

"Where is this transaction and where is that spirituality too,
Where is the happiness and where is the sorrow, for me, who
never needs to analyze it."

Quite often, the routine transactional life of an individual is considered as a hindrance to his spiritual progress. Falling prey to this notion, many spiritual seekers tend to stay away from the routine transactional life and prefer to stay in seclusion to calm their mind in order to achieve spiritual realization.

Janaka, having come out of the spell of ignorance, and having realized that he is the eternal and formless existence, saw the duel of transactional life and spiritual practices as two sides of the same coin; and he realized that both of them are part of the illusory phenomenon.

External transactions of the body and the internal transactions of the mind, both became part of the *seen phenomenon* for him, while he remained as the witness to them.

Verse 20.11

"Where is the illusion and where is the world too. Where is the
affection and where is the renunciation,
Where is this individual and where is that absolute, for the pure
me."

The world - with all its illusions - vanished from his sight, in the sense that he no longer got affected by it. He simply stayed as the *existent being*, and remained blissful within his realization.

He no more felt the compulsion to reckon himself as *this one* or *that one.*

Verse 20.12

"Where is the *activity* or the *inactivity*, where is the liberation and where is the bondage,
For me, who is a *permanent, indivisible and peaceful being*."

The concepts of *activity* and *inactivity* matter to a person who takes himself as an *individual self*; and so do the concepts of bondage and liberation.

The sense of individuality brings the sense of duality with it. Therefore, the forms of the objects appear as if they are *individual beings* having their own existence.

On the other hand, Janaka realized himself as the *permanent, indivisible and peaceful existence.* As a result, the forms of the objects continued to appear as separated from each other, but he recognized their illusory nature; which rendered them ineffective, from his perspective.

Verse 20.13

"Where is the sermon and where is the scripture, where is the disciple and where is the master,
Where is the goal for me, who is the formless *Shiva*."

The master-disciple relationship is a part of the phenomenal world. Knowledge, given through the sermon or through the scriptures, is also a part of the phenomenal world.

Since Janaka realized the illusory nature of the phenomenal world, these concepts didn't hold relevance for him any longer.

He could not see any goal for himself in the phenomenal world since he realized himself as *pure consciousness* – the formless *Shiva*.

Verse 20.14

"Where is the *presence* and where is the *absence*, where is the *one* and where are the *two*;
Why to say more, nothing arises for *me*."

The often-debated ideas such as the *presence* and the *absence* did not matter to Janaka any longer because he realized that these ideas remain confined to the mental constructs; and all the mental constructs are as illusory as the very appearance of the phenomenal world.

Therefore, for him, from his own perspective, nothing really aroused and nothing really set; not any longer.

Only one thing remained – the formless existence, the pure being, the *real self*.

Prostrations

Prostrations to the existence, the one and only.
Prostrations to Ashtavakra, the sage of sages.
Prostrations to Janaka, the wise one amongst spiritual seekers.

Appendix

Indian Philosophy

There are twelve major systems of Indian spiritual philosophy. These systems are broadly divided into two categories:
1.*Believer philosophies.*
2.*Non-Believer philosophies.*

The believer philosophies consider the holy scriptures of Vedas as evidential; whereas the non-believer philosophies do not consider the Vedas as evidential.

In order to show us the path to liberation, these philosophies attempt to determine the nature of three factors:
1.*Individual soul*
2.*God/Existence*
3.*Material world*

Here is a list of these philosophies:

<u>Non-believer philosophies:</u>
1.Charvaka philosophy
2.Buddhism I: Madhyamika philosophy

3.Buddhism II: Yogachari philosophy
4.Buddhism III: Sautantrika
5.Buddhism IV: Vaibhashika
6.Jainism (Arhat Philosophy)

Believer Philosophies:
1.Nyaya philosophy
2.Vaisheshika philosophy
3.Purva-Mimansa philosophy
4.Sankhya philosophy
5.Yoga philosophy
6.Vedanta philosophy: The term *Vedanta* implies *the culmination of the holy scriptures of Vedas.*
Vedanta is the knowledge portion of the *Vedas.*

The teachings of *Vedanta* have been interpreted in three different ways by three different scholars namely Madhvacharya, Ramanujacharya and Adi Shankaracharya; and these interpretations gave rise to three different schools of thought:

1.The *Dualistic interpretation by Madhvacharya:*

An individual soul is considered to be a separate reality from the all-pervasive existence.

2.The *Qualified Non-Dualistic interpretation by Ramanujacharya:*

An individual soul is considered to be the same as *God* existentially, but at the same time it is considered to be having an individual form of its own.

3.The *Non-Dualistic interpretation by Adi Shankaracharya:*

The all-pervasive - and formless - existence is proclaimed as the only reality, and all the forms are considered as illusory.

No individual soul as such, because the formless existence is considered as the *real self* of all subjects.

Apart from these twelve systems, Indian philosophy has few other systems too, such as: *Nakulish Pashupata philosophy, Shaiva philosophy, Pratyabhijna philosophy (also known as Kashmir Shaivism), and Raseshvara philosophy.*

Glossary

Advaita: The word literally means *'Non-dual'*. The philosophy of *Advaita* is based on the knowledge portion of *Vedas*. These knowledge portions are also called *'Upanishads'* or *'Vedanta'*. In these scriptures, individuality of the soul is refuted, and an all-pervasive formless existence is proclaimed as *the only reality*.

Gita: The word literally means *'A Song'*. It typically consists of verses.

Hermitage: A secluded residence or private retreat.

Himalayas: The mountain range spread across northern parts of India, Bhutan & Nepal. Since ancient times, the *Himalayas*, with its spectacular grandeur, have attracted many spiritual people, yogis and even other tourists. Large parts of it are covered with snow throughout the year. This mountain range is spiritually vibrant.

Mortals: Beings which are subject to death.

Sanskrit: An ancient Indian language. It is the most scientific language in the world. Most of the ancient Indian scriptures were written in Sanskrit.

Shiva: The literal meaning is *'He who brings auspiciousness'*. The name of a Hindu God.

Subjective enlightenment: Enlightenment of oneself within oneself.

Tantra: A ritualistic approach towards the spiritual ecstasy, which involves practice such as worship of a deity, repetition of an esoteric syllable, etc.

Vedanta: Knowledge portion of the holy scriptures of *Vedas*. Also known as *'Upanishadas'*.

Vedas: These scriptures serve as the ultimate evidence for many of the Hindus. The *Vedas* are considered as impersonal evidence, and the final authority in the matters of religion and spirituality.

Yoga: A spiritual approach that can be classified as *Rajyoga* and *Hathayoga*. Both are meant for spiritual enlightenment through the practice of restraint of the mind-stuff.

Index

Other Books By Harsha

For updates on Harsha's books, stay tuned at: www.ajatsrishti.com

A Ajat Srishti
THE UNBORN WORLD

Printed in Great Britain
by Amazon

47774789R10138